Washington DISCARD Public Librar
Centerville Library
Centerville, Ohio

# Prologue

How does one fully explain the symbiotic relationship between dog handlers and their dogs? Officers and their dogs mesh into a solid unit that thinks and anticipates as one as they communicate many times in unspoken words. By necessity, theirs is an extremely tight bond. This book is a window into those relationships and the lives of K-9s. It showcases fifteen memorable police and search and rescue dogs and presents their unforgettable stories. A twenty-year search for the most heart-warming stories provides a chronicle that gives insight into an often personal world the public seldom sees. Meet K-9 Argus who against all odds searched for an abandoned newborn in the rugged Canadian wilderness. K-9 Alley of Maryland whose own pain never stopped her from searching for Pentagon victims of 9/11 and K-9 Sirius of the New York Port Authority, the only dog lost at the World Trade Center, will both be remembered for their heroism. K-9 Major from Minnesota and K-9 Luke II from Ohio, two of the most unlikely dogs to reach the pinnacle of success, exemplify the dedication and superb training necessary to assure a place on the often-mean streets to protect the public. The loss of a valued police dog, K-9 Ingo from T⌐        ⌐e, and the hazards military working dogs such         ⌐ry day in foreign lands, bring a whol         d their handlers. And as one Ohio dog         ⌐, sometimes the most successful dog ꓵ        ꓵog" mold. The story of these dogs and many         ꓵold with poignancy and sometime humor clearing up any misconceptions anyone might have about the nature and duties of today's K-9s. A must read for anyone who has ever loved a dog.

Centerville Library
Washington-Centerville Public Library
Centerville, Ohio

# *Badge on My Collar*

## A Chronicle of Courageous Canines

by

Marilyn Jeffers Walton

authorHOUSE®

*AuthorHouse™*
*1663 Liberty Drive, Suite 200*
*Bloomington, IN 47403*
*www.authorhouse.com*
*Phone: 1-800-839-8640*

*© 2007 Marilyn Jeffers Walton. All rights reserved.*

*No part of this book may be reproduced, stored in a retrieval system, or transmitted by any means without the written permission of the author.*

*First published by AuthorHouse 12/14/2007*

*ISBN: 978-1-4343-4186-0 (sc)*

*Printed in the United States of America*
*Bloomington, Indiana*

*This book is printed on acid-free paper.*

*Cover photograph, Levi, courtesy of Jan Ballard*

*Additional cover photography by R. Harold and Carolyn G. Kramer*

*Photograph on spine -- Sandy*

*Unless otherwise stated, all photos are courtesy of individual dog handlers.*

# Dedication

For the brave police, military and search and rescue dog handlers who give their dedicated and unselfish service and for their faithful four-legged companions that remain steadfast at their sides. And in appreciation for the four-thousand dogs that went off to Vietnam with their valiant soldiers. Of that number, only two-hundred war dogs came home.

# Acknowledgements

Carolyn and Harold Kramer
Patrol Officer Vince Lovejoy & K-9 Ki'
Patrol Officer Shawn Terrell & K-9 Simon
Patrol Officer David King & K-9 Dover
Patrol Officer Greg Stidd & K-9 Dutch
Patrol Officer Andy Warrick & K-9 Bomber
Patrol Officer James Bodner & Sabre
Patrol Officer Todd Mann
Laura Vokoun
Phyllis Greer
Dawn Nesja
Alice Hanan
Trudy Pollok
Lawrence Aimoe
Dan Battistone
Mario Siciliano
Grant Mitchell
Jill Schmidt
Marc Drummond

# Table of Contents

# Foreword

The highest duty a police dog can do is the giving of his life for his handler or another person. The dog is trained to respond and to give his life if need be. Officers who have trained dogs believe that the dogs understand this, and if they could respond in any other way, they would not. Unswerving loyalty and dedication, a determined instinct to please, and faith in a trusted companion are their universal traits. Praise is their highest reward. It is said that while on duty, police officers daily fight a war. There is no one else these K-9 officers would choose to accompany them into battle than their devoted and courageous four-legged partners.

*Russell D. Hess*

National Executive Director and past President of
the United States Police Canine Association, Inc.

# Sorter

A dog sat in a wooden box along with forty-nine other dogs in boxes by the seashore guarding the town of Corinth. In the dark of night the enemy arrived to invade the town. All but one of the dogs, Sorter, was slain as the enemy advanced to the town. Tired and wounded, the dog fled to the town to give warning.

The town was successfully defended by its people.

"To him alone were the honors of victory," said the people.

They presented the dog with a collar. The inscription read:

*"Sorter, Defender and Savior of Corinth"*

A monument was erected in his honor and as a tribute to the other forty-nine canine heroes who fell.

The year was 431 B.C.

Many dogs followed demonstrating Sorter's bravery and steadfast allegiance.

Today we call them K-9s.

# Preface

When a person walks into a room and smells a pot of vegetable soup cooking, that person would smell only the soup. When a K-9 walks into the same room, he isolates every ingredient with his sensitive nose.

A K-9's nose is hundreds of times more sensitive than a human's. A K-9 can find what he is looking for in a box of black pepper hidden inside a container of mothballs. Whatever he is looking for can be soaked in gasoline or covered with strong onions. He'll find it just the same. His sophisticated sense of smell is greater than a scientific instrument, and his hearing is twenty times better than our own. Those qualities make him extremely valuable to police departments and search and rescue organizations. The dog's instinct to seek and find, his fierce and protective loyalty and his ability to control his aggression, all combine to make him a perfect partner. He is a deterrent to crime, and his presence often means gun shots will not have to be fired.

When trying to find a partner, a police officer will most likely look for a one- to two-year old male dog. The males tend to be bigger, more outgoing and more curious. However, female dogs have been used, and one, Tangie, was the first non-human member of the Women Peace Officers Association in California.

If a dog is offered to a police department, an officer knowledgeable of dog behavior would visit to evaluate the dog and look for specific characteristics. An officer unknown to the dog might come up behind it and pull its back leg to see how the dog reacts. The dog must respond with some aggression. He cannot appear to be indifferent or scared. If he passes the test, he has the chance to go on to K-9 school.

While training for fourteen weeks, the dog must not fight with the other dogs. He cannot be afraid of loud noises. He must be able to tolerate gunfire and not shy away. The dog needs a strong retrieval instinct, that is, the innate drive to go find whatever the officer wants to find. Collectively, such traits will earn him high marks.

As the dog trains, he is matched with an officer who has been waiting for a dog. The dog learns the basic police commands and that he must only obey his officer. Soon he learns that when an officer commands "Out!" the dog is to stop whatever he is doing immediately. So that the dog can never be poisoned, he is taught never to accept anything to eat from anyone but the officer.

When a dog completes the intense training, a graduation ceremony is held. The well-trained dog becomes an integral part of the often complex world of crime control. For K-9 officers, their proudest moment after graduation is the dog's first "street apprehension" when the untested animal chases and catches his first criminal. It is a time when he proves himself and his abilities and, therefore, his value to the department. An enthusiastic dog sitting tall in the back seat of a cruiser is a constant deterrent to potential lawbreakers when that dog is on duty.

K-9s are utilized in a variety of ways. Most of the time police departments use them as patrol dogs that vigilantly look for criminals and search buildings. Some dogs have even "testified" in court cases. The dogs are commonly used to sniff out "contraband" with their powerful noses identifying substances that are illegal such as narcotics, explosives or accelerants used to start fires. There is an ever-increasing need for such dogs at airports and in the military to enhance security. Some very specialized dogs are used to find dead bodies. Most dogs are cross-trained to perform more than one function.

Dedicated search and rescue dogs and police dogs also find lost people. Should an elderly or confused person or a child ever become lost, there's a good chance that a searching K-9 will find them.

A misconception among some people is that police dogs are trained to kill. But, they are not vicious, and they bite only when they are ordered to pursue and hold a suspect that has refused to obey a K-9 officer's orders. The dogs are trained only to hold a fleeing suspect until the officer arrives for the arrest. A dog with a

***Author receives a K-9 kiss.***
Courtesy of R. Harold and Carolyn G. Kramer

biting temperament would "flunk out" of K-9 school. If the suspect is cooperative, a dog will only hold until the handler commands, "Out!" The dog's jaw pressure is felt at one thousand pounds per square inch, equivalent to resting the front wheel of a compact car on one's arm.

Once a K-9 catches a suspect, he will not back down. That goes against his training. If the arresting officer tells him to "watch" a suspect, the dog will sit or "down" staying alert as he stares into the suspect's face until the officer releases him from his duties. That could be two minutes or three days. It makes no difference to the dog. He's just doing his job.

K-9s work only to please their officers. Their best reward for a job well done is a kind word of praise, playing with a favorite toy or a good scratch on the ears. At the end of a work shift, the skilled dog that can be worth $5000 to more than $25,000 to a police department goes home to live with his officer. The dog coming home after work acts more like the family pet when he's off duty. At home, he may romp with the officer's children or get into the trash the way any pet might do. But a police dog always knows the difference between on and off-duty.

To help keep a dog's skills sharp most police K-9s compete against each other annually to determine which dog will become "Top Dog of the Year." It is the highest honor for just one dog in the country. Individual and regional teams are also chosen for special recognition as "Top Teams."

Because of the exhilaration of the job, most police dogs work for only seven or eight years. Each time the car races and the siren wails the dogs become very excited, and after years of service in the fast-paced world of police pursuits, the dogs must retire. As the dog starts slowing down, and once keen senses start to weaken, retirement is anticipated. When that time comes, the dog spends his final years with the officer at home. Retiring a dog from service is one of the hardest things a police officer must do.

When private citizens turn out their lights and go to sleep each night, they can rest assured that throughout the night and into the early morning hours, thousands of police dogs across the country are on patrol. Ears pricked up to listen, noses high in the air, the brave police dog is tireless in his effort to protect the public. Any officer who works with a dog will tell you, "He's the best partner I've ever had."

The true value of the police dog was tested once when a Michigan officer arrived at the scene of a restaurant break-in. The burglar was still inside.

"Come out!" ordered the officer.

The burglar remained inside.

"I'm going to send the K-9 in to get you out," the officer warned, as he radioed for a K-9 unit.

But all the K-9s were busy at other locations.

The officer could not wait. With his head thrown back and with his most fearsome tone, the officer imitated the loud bark of a police dog.

The burglar came out with his hands up.

Such is the reputation of the K-9.

Throughout the world, the descendents of Sorter, just as loyal and just as brave, continue his noble tradition.

*King and Andy*

# K-9 King
## "The Children's Angel"

Before K-9 King went to work, police dogs were seldom used in the State of Minnesota. The City of Anoka decided to try a dog on their police force, so in 1967 local community service groups combined their money with the police department to purchase King for $780.

Full-grown, King arrived in Anoka one frigid and snowy day about the same time a young man named Andy Revering was just returning from the military where he had worked with sentry dogs. Andy and his wife had no children of their own yet. King became their first "child."

Andy and King left for the National Police Dog Academy in Moline, Kansas, and for fourteen weeks they trained. Besides learning his official police duties, King was trained to never hurt children even if they would reach out towards him. He learned all his lessons well and soon graduated.

The first time Andy took King to visit a school he noticed something special. Each time King finished performing for the children, he could not wait to go out into the crowd to greet them. There was no holding King back when it came to children. While many police dogs are kept on a leash to visit, King was un-snapped from his leash to freely wade into the sea of smiling children. He seemed to personally greet each child, accepting their hugs as though

**King, on the left, sitting by Duke who joined the
Anoka Police Department two years later**

he was each child's family pet. He waited patiently as everyone had a turn to hug his strong neck. King blissfully enjoyed the feel of the anxious small hands that patted his broad back and furry head. The same cool alert eyes that watched prisoners in the police car turned bright and loving as King ran from child to child. He had a special place in his heart for children from the very start, and over his years of service the whole community knew it.

King was the youngest, toughest, fastest and most of the time, gentlest member of the police force. The children of Anoka closely followed his exciting adventures.

One night King was called upon to locate a man who had fled after wounding two other men with a gun after an argument. Sirens screamed in the night as Andy and King, along with other police officers, chased the man. After the suspect's car got stuck in a ditch, he jumped and ran into the woods in a grove of trees laced with tall swamp grass.

So that no one could see him, the man threw himself to the ground and lay face down, perfectly silent and trying not to move.

All was deathly quiet but for the chirp of crickets that still night.

Hidden in the swamp grass, the suspect held his guns and waited.

"Can't see him anywhere," said Andy, as he led King through the thick grass.

But furry cop could.

In that instant, King emitted a fearsome growl and charged ahead. Diving into the swamp grass, King wrestled ferociously with the suspect. Time and time again, the man thrashed and rolled in the grass trying to break loose from King's firm grip, but the dog's strong jaws held the suspect's leg tightly.

"Get him off me, get him off!" the frantic man yelled.

But King would not get off. Inch by inch, he tugged the man almost ten feet from where the guns were dropped before the dog would let go. By separating the man from his guns, King saved Andy's life. King was, indeed, a true hero. All the children that King visited at schools eagerly read about his heroic deed in the newspapers.

Because of his heroism, King was one day brushed and groomed to make his first television appearance on the children's show Clancy and Carmen, where he received the Lassie Gold Award presented by the producer of the Lassie Show. The award was presented to him for his act of outstanding heroism and devotion.

But King was not done amazing children yet.

Sometime later King was called to action again when desperate parents called the police department to report that their ten-year-old daughter, Tammy, had disappeared. Her father had put her to bed at 9 o'clock and later went to bed himself. When Tammy's mother came home from working late that night, she went in to check on her daughter and found her gone.

It was a crisp clear night when the increasingly colder air predicted the coming of a harsh Minnesota winter. Andy snapped King's tracking leash to his collar and left for Tammy's home where her mother gave Andy a shirt the young girl had recently worn. He held the shirt down to King's level, and the dog sniffed the shirt methodically with his sensitive nose. Now, he had her scent.

King trotted out in front of Andy in the darkness leading the way on his long leather leash. When Andy and King had gone about three-hundred yards, King turned toward a nearby park. He pricked up his ears and began to pant. Andy could feel the leash tighten as King suddenly moved faster and more excitedly.

Then the panting stopped.

King stood still and thrust his muzzle upward into the cool night air. He pulled it all in through his nose. Andy knew when King stopped panting he had found what he was looking for.

There, near a swimming pool building, King saw a sleeping figure and gently approached her. At his feet was Tammy, still in her pajamas, wrapped in a blanket and clutching two dolls. King gently poked his cold nose into the little girl's side. She awoke and patted him on the head. King sniffed her sleepy face and gave her a big lick on the cheek.

Tammy later admitted she had had an argument with her mother and wanted to worry her a little. The next day she happily posed for pictures with King and thanked him for finding her. Once again, King was a hero in the eyes of Anoka's children.

One night when Andy and King were off duty, Andy put King in his dog kennel in the backyard of the house. King's kennel was adjacent to the church that sat just beyond Andy's yard. It was a quiet winter night, and snow as light as fluttering feathers was softly falling.

"Good night, King," Andy said affectionately, ruffling the dog's warm fur with his large hand.

Andy went into the house and went to bed.

But soon King started to bark. It was 3 o'clock in the morning, and the dog was very restless.

Andy raised the window and looked out. He could see nothing.

"Quiet!" he called to King.

Half an hour later King awoke Andy again with an inquisitive growl that graduated to a prolonged and alarmed bark. Andy could see nothing in the yard. He could see no lights or movement anywhere—just the gentle falling of quiet snowflakes on the moonlit yard.

"Be quiet, King!" he called again.

Throughout the night, King paced and barked. Something was upsetting him terribly.

By morning the call came in.

School children walking past the church in the morning found a laundry basket on the church steps. Snuggled inside was a baby wrapped in a blanket.

The helpless baby had been born during the night and placed in the basket by its confused mother. The people at the church cared for the fragile cold infant that King had always known was there.

No matter how quiet the mother had tried to be, King had known her secret all along. Now, there would be another child in Anoka for him to protect.

By then, the Reverings had children of their own, and King spent many happy hours by their sides.

King had many children to care for, but the children on his street were his favorites. In a state where many feet of snow remain on the ground for months, King needed a sled. So Andy had a wooden sled and fine harness made for the playful dog.

***King had a special place in his heart for children.***

King's well-used sled was a favorite of the neighborhood children. During his off-duty hours, King was fastened to the sled and spent his afternoons pulling it up and down the street.

In the sub-zero cold of Minnesota's winters, wearing only his dark fur coat, King made regular stops on the street to pick up the children and race them swiftly through the deep snow. Icy crystals from condensed breath crusted on his chin and whiskers and a mantle of soft snow clung to the fur on his back.

For many years, King heard the joyful children laughing and shrieking behind him on the sled. As the neighborhood children

***Off duty but still on guard***

grew, their younger brothers and sisters called King's name as they took their turns in his sled.

But as the children grew, the echoes of their jubilant squeals became memories melting away in the thaw of many springs. King grew older and more tired and soon reached retirement age. There would be no more wild rides for the children on his sled as King faced the winter of his own years. The steady rhythm of his footpads fell silent on the street.

By then, Andy had become Chief of Police.

***King's well-used sled was a favorite of the neighborhood children.***

"When King retires, he'll have a broken heart," Andy said ruefully.

In 1974, King was fully retired from service. He died of natural causes the following year at the Chief's home.

The impact this fearless protector had on Anoka's citizens will not soon be forgotten. Even after thirty years, a cartoon image of King is still used on educational materials passed out to school children.

In 1977, a small children's park in the city was dedicated and named King Memorial Park. A life-sized cement statue of King with a bronze plaque in his honor sat there for ten years. At its unveiling, school children recited essays on the value of dogs.

After ten years, the statue became worn from all the children's hugs and pats. It was replaced by a bronze exact likeness of King done from a photograph.

In 1993 Andy welcomed a special visitor to Anoka. Television star, Rin Tin Tin, traveled the country promoting his show, "Rin Tin Tin, K-9 Cop." When he stopped in Anoka to also promote the police-sponsored D.A.R.E. anti-drug program, the Anoka K-9s put on a demonstration. Rin Tin Tin's trainer was so impressed with them that she brought the television star to King Memorial Park for photographs with the statue of King, Anoka's famous first police dog and historically, one of Anoka's canine finest.

*King, Rin Tin Tin and Chief Revering*

Each icy winter, Artic winds blow in from Canada and swirl around the statue of King, covering it in a soft blanket of snow. Winter melts into spring, and later the dazzling sunshine of bright summer days reflects off Minnesota's 10,000 lakes. Through it all, K-9 King, steadfast sentinel, watches over the children of Anoka who play beneath him in the park. It is his final and most satisfying assignment.

# K-9 Major
# "Unchained Fury"

One bitter Minnesota day in a blinding snowstorm a young dog was born in a snow bank. The only puppy to survive, he nuzzled against his mother for warmth and protection from the cruel wind.

As he grew, he was given to a rural Minnesota farm family who eventually came to fear him. Major was chained to a stake on their rundown farm. As the biting winter wind howled across the plain, lonely Major survived each day without a doghouse. As a snowy lump of fur, he hunkered down against the cold. He had no one to play with, and he trusted no one. Major suffered through the hard winter with ragged frostbitten ears. He was sickly and thin, and children with sticks teased the pitiful dog even when he tried to eat his meager dinner. He never forgot it. Years later, he would still distance himself from children.

When Officer Janet Koch of the Eden Prairie Police Department was told about him, she decided to visit since she was looking for a police partner. Perhaps Major would be that special dog she was looking for.

When Janet visited the dog, she crept up to him slowly. She peeked at him from behind the trees to test his reactions. Major growled and barked ferociously. Despite his unfriendly nature, Janet slowly inched closer. Suddenly, the dog's fierceness eased. As she finally got close enough to stroke him with her gentle hand, Major's heart melted. She felt an instant bond with the dog and arranged with his owners to take him home that day. She unhooked Major from his dreaded stake and led him to her car. With great enthusiasm, Janet drove directly to the sheriff's office to show off her new dog.

Major was a bold dog, and he strutted right into the building. Finding no one in the sheriff's office, Janet left Major there and closed the door. When the sheriff returned, startled Major leapt from the floor, jumped over the desk and chased him out of his own office and down the hall.

Janet laughed as she chased and then caught the energetic dog. It was time to take him home. Janet's home was the first true home he had known. She tenderly fed him a bowl of warm cooked rice and cottage cheese. Major savored each bite, enjoying his meal in peaceful surroundings far from his desolate farmyard. For the first time someone cared for him. That night, Major bounded onto Janet's waterbed and curled up next to her, touching his thick bristly outdoor coat to her back.

*For a lonely farm dog--a dream come true*

*Major's new home came complete with a
new friend, Fancy, to play with.*

Slowly, Major overcame his physical problems, gained weight
and regained his health. For all the hardships the dog had had in
the first two years of life, he still kept heart and courage. He was
so grateful to Janet for saving him and offering him a happy home,
he would do anything for her. Whenever anyone, friend or relative,
came near Janet or tried to touch her, Major ran to her side and
offered his protection. It was a habit he never broke.

When Major's training began, he was a natural. The curious dog
watched as Janet slipped on a heavily-padded sleeve. When she told
Major to grab it, he responded like he had done it all his life. When
she taught him new commands, he did everything right on the first
try. He was the easiest dog Janet ever trained.

When she took him in the car, Major stared at the ignition with
quizzical eyes waiting for her to insert the key. Then he looked at
the brake pedal anticipating that she would step on it. As she did,

13

***It took Major just three minutes to find this gun in high grass.***

his eyes moved to the gearshift and then the steering wheel. Without her realizing it, Major had learned the sequential steps to start and drive the car.

With his new-found freedom, Major developed a fondness for chasing and catching skunks much to Janet's dismay. No matter how many times he was "skunked," he still pursued them. In his old surroundings, they had always been just beyond his reach. With no stake to hold him, he was now free to initiate the chase.

Soon, Janet and Major were official police partners patrolling Minnesota's streets. Late one night they stopped at a location where two drunken loggers were fighting in the street.

*The new partners take to the road.*

*Janet and Major*

"Break it up and go home!" Janet ordered from the safety of her car.

But as she tried to drive away, one of the men clung to her partially-opened car window and was dragged along. Janet slammed on the brakes and radioed for help. She stepped out to arrest the drunken men, leaving Major in the car. Then a struggle broke out. Major barked frantically as he watched helplessly from the car. He knew how to start and drive the car but not how to get out of it.

Janet had just clicked one handcuff on the first man's wrist when the second man sneaked up behind her and grabbed for her gun. When she whirled around to stop him, the first man slashed at her with the dangling handcuffs. Immediately, she sprayed the men with mace and ran for her car to release Major.

"I'm not afraid of that dog!" the drunken man roared.

But he should have been. With tremendous speed and ferocity, Major leapt up, knocked him down and held him there until officers arrived to make arrests.

"You never would have got me without that dog!" the man bellowed as he was dragged away.

The next day, Janet saw one of the men at the police station where he was being held. Now he was sober and calm.

"That's some dog you've got," he said happily, "Can I pet him?"

Major's memory and instinct served him well, and he chose not to be petted by anyone who would try to harm Janet and let the man know it.

After many routine nights on patrol, Janet got a call to locate a very troubled man who had escaped from a mental hospital in Wisconsin. He drove for four hours into Minnesota and abandoned his car. He had been ingesting powerful prescription medicine and illegal drugs that combined to make him agitated, confused and very strong.

The gravel crunched beneath Janet's tires as she drove slowly at the road's edge in the darkness. Suddenly she spotted the man wandering around a busy highway. When he saw her car, he panicked and ran. Janet and Major continued their pursuit. They followed the fleeing man into the countryside. Janet stopped the car, and she and Major got out. The night was misty and silent as all alone they cautiously trudged through the thick brush listening for any movement. The sound of Major's fast panting broke the dead silence.

Visibility was poor making it hard to locate the man. They paused momentarily to listen again. They heard nothing.

Just then, in one terrorizing moment, the deranged man suddenly sprang out in the darkness and punched Janet behind the ear causing her to fall to the ground and briefly pass out. He hovered above her dangerously. Instinctively, Major sank his sharp teeth into the man and shook him back and forth violently. Major was growling viciously and attacking with fury when Janet came to.

To defend himself, the man grabbed Major by the neck with his powerful hands and started to choke the fighting dog. The gripping hands were unbelievably strong. Major struggled and thrashed about wildly gasping for air, but he could fight no more and soon lost consciousness. Janet garnered every ounce of strength she had left and wrestled with the man until Major came to. The bewildered animal staggered around for a moment in confusion. Through dazed eyes he saw the man over-powering Janet. The attacker grabbed for Janet's handcuffs, her gun and her nightstick. With renewed strength and raging fury, Major attacked again. Just as he lunged at the man's chest, Janet simultaneously reached her hand up between the man and the dog. Before he could stop himself, Major accidentally bit Janet's hand.

"Major!" she yelled in searing pain.

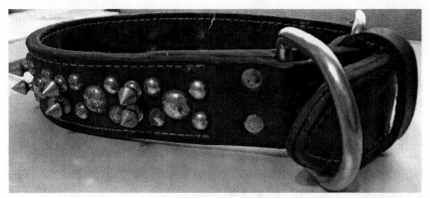

**Major's spiked collar**

Major was so upset he opened his mouth and froze. In that brief instant the man whirled around and grabbed his neck again. Janet used every weapon she had to successfully overpower the man, and the battle was over. Although she was exhausted, Janet spoke soothing soft words to the man to keep him calm.

Police officers arrived, and Janet was taken to the hospital to be treated for an injured arm and a dog bite. She knew that the bite had been her fault and not Major's and hoped he knew it too. She vowed that night that in the future no one would ever have the opportunity to choke her dog. Trotting along proudly afterward, Major sported a collar studded with sharp silver spikes to prevent anyone from ever grabbing his vulnerable neck again.

Even when he required veterinary care Major wanted only Janet to touch him. Upon one occasion, after his powerful protests knocked one veterinarian across the room, a sign was placed on his cage:

"DO NOT TOUCH THIS DOG!"

With or without his spiked collar, Major had his way.

Since Major also had bomb detection capability, he was allowed to fly in the front cabin of airliners with Janet. On his flights, Major curled up at Janet's feet and waited for the flight attendants to bring him his own tray. Far above the farm where he was born, Major felt the excitement of take-offs, and he logged many miles of domestic travel. Passengers often mistook him for a seeing-eye dog since Janet dressed in plainclothes, and they were quite puzzled when she pulled out a book to read.

Between flights, Major wandered through the airports on a lead. Even when Janet went into the restroom, he felt he must watch out for her, and the protective dog slunk along under the row of stalls poking his furry head under each door to greet many a startled woman.

In the years that followed, Major served both his partner and the Eden Prairie and Minnetonka Police Departments admirably. During his long career, he once hit on $1,200,000 in cash drug money at the airport. A box had been seized there, and the call came for Major to come sniff it to confirm its contents. Major confirmed all suspicions, and the box was forfeited. Later, the confiscated money was divided between several police departments. The find meant $250,000 came to Janet's department and later funded a new training facility.

As Major began to show his age, he was retired from service. A second dog, Levi, took his place. In his cozy home aging Major slept fitfully behind Janet's front door awaiting her footsteps every day. When she was safely home from work, Major slept a deep and peaceful sleep.

In the waning years of his life, retired Major played in his leisure hours. On warm days, he contented himself chewing on a fine hunk of wood. On cold days he eagerly took the snow shovel Janet bought for him so he would stop trying to take hers. From a distance, wary children watched as Major joyfully scooped up piles of snow and playfully flipped the cold white powder that long ago had stung his tender ears. It fell harmlessly onto his back and covered Janet's freshly-shoveled driveway. It was his enemy no more. For nearly fourteen years Major was Janet's companion. Gradually he began to

*Happy and content*

*The snow was his enemy no more.*

lose his sight, and the once frost-bitten ears could no longer hear.

Major's police career was an illustrious one. He was Top Dog in the nation in 1981 and came back to win again in 1982 making Janet Koch the first female member to compete in the United States Police Canine Association trials and the first to win so many times. Today, she is one of the most respected dog trainers in the country. Under her tutelage, Major was not only National Champion in 1981 and 1982 at the National Police Canine Field Trials, but in 1983 and 1984, he and Janet took First Place as National Police Canine Team and Third

*A true champion*

***Testimony to love and good training***

***Immensely proud***

Place Overall. In 1984 Major was Regional Champion and placed fourth overall. At each regional competition to qualify for Nationals, Major bested sixty dogs, and at Nationals he competed against up to another one hundred and ten dogs. If a price could have been put on Major's value, it would have been well over $25,000.

From a shabby rural farm dog, unchained Major started on the bottom and finished as a top cop. It is love that drove him.

The compassion of one woman removed him from a world of harshness and boredom and enabled him to live a good life. Major sped along in cars and flew across the country. His life was rich with love, companionship and excitement. And at the end of a distinguished career, the previously neglected dog always returned to the one thing that had always been most elusive to him--a warm place called home.

*A legend among police dogs*

# K-9 Ingo
## "Valor and Sacrifice"

There is a kennel in Bowling Green, Kentucky, where noble dogs are born. It was there that Officer Allen Herald first saw little ten-week-old Ingo. Allen played with the active pup that licked his face, and the puppy had a new home. Allen bought the dog for a pet, but later when he decided to join the K-9 Division of the Metropolitan Police Department in Nashville, Tennessee, he donated the dog to the department so that the two could work together on the force.

When Ingo was three months old and already thirty-five pounds, Allen taught him to do a "running attack." The young dog ran full speed ahead to grab the pant leg of any perceived "bad guy," and he held it tightly to fight the battle for Allen. Many of the men who worked with Allen on a second job he held ended up with tattered and frayed pant legs as Ingo pursued his imagined prey. Once when left home alone with Allen's wife, Gwen, Ingo chased her as she ran to answer the phone. She had to climb up on a chair to get him to let go of her pants. The dog never tired of the game. Afterward, he ran laps around the couch and tore through the house knocking over whatever stood in his path. Anything or anyone who stood in Ingo's path had reason to fear.

When puppyhood ended, Ingo completed K-9 school and was taken to explosive detection training. For eight-hours a day, five-days a week, Ingo honed his bomb-detection skills. For training,

Allen removed Ingo's metal choke chain and slipped a special leather bomb collar around his neck. Ingo learned to associate the collar with his new task and knew that every time he wore the collar he was to sniff for bombs.

First, Allen used an acrid black powder that Ingo had never smelled before. He put it on the floor so that the dog could locate and smell the nitrate, the chemical used in most bombs. To start, Allen led Ingo around the room on a leash.

"Seek!" he called, as he pointed to the black powder.

The moment Ingo sniffed it, Allen told him to sit. Over and over again, Ingo was rewarded with bits of food or a throw of his favorite ball as he consistently sniffed the powder and sat. He very quickly learned to associate the smell of the powder with food or play.

As Ingo progressed, Allen switched the black powder with other explosive substances that were harder to smell. Instead of hiding them low to the ground, he hid them high up or sometimes in suitcases. Often, he took the pages out of a book and hid bags of the explosives between the book covers. Then Ingo would have to find it, even though it was far up in a bookcase.

Once Ingo learned to identify all the chemicals, he was taken to the airport and taught to search airplanes by running down the aisle seeking the smell of nitrate. In between, and up and over the seats Ingo scrambled as he searched. If the powder was hidden in an overhead storage bin, Ingo jumped up in the seat below it and quickly sat down just like a passenger.

By graduation day, Ingo could even detect plastic bombs having little scent. Not only did he sit when he found explosives, but he always backed up three steps seeming to sense danger. Allen sensed that Ingo understood, and three steps backward signaled peril.

Ingo was soon being called to duty whenever someone phoned in a bomb threat. Frequently, he was called to the airport where he

*Ingo's reward was his favorite ball.*

***Allen and Ingo***

searched normal airliners, the private plane of Jesse Jackson and the planes of dignitaries from foreign countries.

One day, Ingo was called to the famous Opryland Hotel to search the room of visitor President Ronald Reagan. He strutted through the grand entrance over plush carpet and past the splashing indoor fountains and waterfalls. Ingo entered the President's suite of rooms and searched under beds and behind couches. Only when the dog was sure the room was safe would the President be allowed to enter.

After finding the suite safe, Ingo left.

Not long afterward, Allen's phone rang, and the Secret Service called him and Ingo back to the hotel. When the pair arrived, they were taken to one of the rooms of the presidential suite. With great drama and concern, one of the men pointed to a dog mess left on the floor of the room.

"Did your dog do THIS in the President's room?" the agent asked indignantly.

Allen was the first to defend his dog, saying that Ingo had not done such a thing. Unable to remain serious any longer, the agents began to laugh. Then one bent over and picked up the plastic pile he had put there to play a joke on Allen and the accomplished bomb dog.

For three years, Ingo served as the county's only bomb dog. When there were no bomb threats, he rode on regular patrol to find "bad guys," and flew above Nashville in police helicopters.

His days were not without hazards. Ingo once fell down a flight of steps while chasing a suspect involved in a drug store burglary and was rushed to the veterinarian's. Allen scrubbed with the vet to stay by his dog's side as a bone fragment was removed from Ingo's elbow. All patched up, the dog soon returned to patrol.

Each night, as Ingo and Allen left for work, Allen's two-year-old daughter, Brittany, patted the dog she called "Auno." After his nightly pat, Ingo leapt into the patrol car and started the 10:30 p.m. shift.

**Ready for patrol**

*Helicopter patrol*

After a few hours on patrol, Allen and Ingo routinely drove through Krystal Hamburgers where they took their dinner break.

Ingo was a dog who loved to eat. He whined and barked at the drive-through window where the employees waited to feed him a warm, juicy hamburger. It was an empty night for the workers and for Ingo if he did not show up for his nightly hamburger. On particularly busy nights, Allen often stopped to buy Ingo a steak for a special reward.

One cold wintry day, shortly before Christmas, Brittany Herald patted Ingo's head as usual and told him good-bye. Nashville's famous bomb dog was called to work on the day shift. The First American Bank in Inglewood, Tennessee, had been held up that morning by an armed bank robber. Afterward, the robber escaped. The smell of bombs was temporarily set aside as Ingo joined other

Tennessee officers tracking the robber. Police sirens wailed, and red lights flashed in the town of Inglewood. Tires spun and squealed as the police cars raced into the parking lot of an apartment building.

Allen jumped out of his cruiser and quickly put Ingo's lead and tracking harness on the excited dog. With another officer behind him as backup, Allen and Ingo started to track the suspect who had been seen running between two apartment buildings.

Ingo sniffed the area and sensed danger. His nose to the ground, he circled.

Then, he took three steps back.

Ingo had found his "bad guy." The robber hid in the stairwell of a breezeway of the apartment building just ahead.

Very slowly and quietly, Allen eased along a wall to look around the corner into the shadowed breezeway.

Suddenly, there was movement in the dark stairwell. A gun pointed right at him.

Ingo saw it too.

Instinctively, Allen jumped back. With great ferocity and speed, Ingo charged in alone around the corner to face the robber who stood in his path. Every minute of K-9 training and the puppy game of running attack was telling him to protect the officer.

CRACK!

A shot fired.

After the momentary blinding flash, Allen looked around the corner again.

The gun was still pointed at him.

Under the stairs, he could see Ingo lying completely still on the ground.

Gunfire rang out a second time, and within minutes the suspect was captured and taken away.

As the arrest was made, Allen ran to his beloved Ingo. He picked up the wounded dog, shot in the head, and rushed him into a waiting police car. Another officer drove. Once again, sirens wailed as all emergency equipment was turned on. The car carrying a wounded and valued officer on the force raced through town to the veterinarian.

But before the car arrived, all was lost.

Ingo died cradled in Allen's arms.

Heartbroken, Allen Herald returned to his Nashville home. It was a home filled with pictures of Ingo and a home full of all the trophies earned by the dog in police dog competitions.

Allen knew in his heart that Ingo had given his own life to save his partner, and it was devastating coming home without him.

***Trophies proudly earned***

The next day the suspect was charged with bank robbery. There was one more charge—killing a police dog.

In just two short hours tragedy was brought to the State of Tennessee. Nashville was in mourning. Ingo's story went out to all the national newspapers, and people who read about Ingo were deeply saddened by his loss.

Four days after Ingo's death a full-scale police funeral took place. Under grey drizzling skies, gauging the mood of the city, a procession of cars slowly left the funeral home where a small white casket had been donated.

*K-9 Ingo – the ultimate sacrifice*

*Final ride*

A line of fifty cars over a mile long, with windshield wipers slapping in unison, wound through the streets of grey Nashville past the police department, past Krystal Hamburgers and past the Metropolitan Justice Center where the suspect waited inside to be tried for his crimes.

***The long funeral procession***

The police cars drove silently with their lights flashing mournfully in the rain. People stopped on the street to watch. At first they smiled as they saw other Tennessee K-9s in their cars excitedly panting, pacing and whining. But when they looked into Allen's car, they saw only a small white casket. People who watched from the streets turned respectfully quiet as the cars passed through town towards the Police Academy, which would be Ingo's final resting place.

Graveside services were held, and the police chaplain spoke of Ingo.

"I hope this will give a greater appreciation for K-9 dogs and for the danger they and their partners face," he said.

*A sorrowful farewell*

*Words from the police chaplain*

***Grieving Allen and his wife, Gwen***

***A quiet and final resting place***

*Allen receives the flag that covered Ingo's casket.*

*Saluting a hero*

Allen choked back tears and hugged his wife. K-9 teams from many police departments stood at attention in hushed silence as Ingo was laid to rest.

Ingo gave the best that he had, and that was his life. The community had lost a valued friend. Ingo was the first police dog to be killed in the line of duty in Nashville. He was honored the following year in the police memorial for officers killed in the line of duty, and he received the "Monza" award from the United States Police Canine Association. It is given to a dog that has given his own life to save his partner. The plaque sat beside Ingo's "Quarter Award" which he was given by the United States Police Canine Association for the first quarter of 1984-85 for his outstanding performance in detection and prevention of crimes after he had tracked for six hours, finally locating a rape suspect.

Five-year-old Ingo had been "just a big family pet" but had been trained into an award-winning police dog that nabbed more than fifty armed robbers and burglars. Nashville was a safer place because of him. Now, the famous bomb dog was gone.

Just after Ingo's death, Allen received flowers, cards and calls from all over the country. A Nashville veterinary group donated $500, the original price of Ingo, as a memorial award in Ingo's name to the police department. The bank that had been robbed offered to buy the Police Canine Division a new dog.

Another offer came on a cold January day from an Oregon trainer who had read Ingo's heroic story. She raised German shepherds and offered to pick out her best for Allen. She reached into a litter of tumbling playful pups and made her choice. The pup she picked stood out because of his alertness and courage. Above all it was important that this dog have courage.

The woman placed the fuzzy puppy in an air carrier and took him aboard a plane headed for Nashville. When the plane landed, she set the carrier down on the floor of the airport and opened it. Out scampered the baby German shepherd.

Allen scooped up thirteen pounds of squirmy, tail-wagging pup that merrily licked his face. Allen felt whole again with a shepherd in his arms. The warm bundle of fur was quickly named Auno by daughter Brittany as she hugged the little pup. Auno would be "her police dog." The Heralds took Auno home.

True to its word, the bank bought a second dog. Within months the same Kentucky kennel that had been Ingo's birthplace sent a three-year-old dog named Onix to Nashville. Allen decided to accept him. The Herald home that had been so empty that sad December day was suddenly alive with German shepherds.

Though one dog had fallen, the desire to protect Allen and exhibit unquestionable courage and valor lived on in the successor. Onix's paws followed in noble footsteps.

Riding, head held high behind Allen in the car, Onix became a constant tribute to Ingo's heroic memory. And in the bright city lights of Nashville and the dark shadows of the hills of Tennessee where hundreds of legends abound, the story of Ingo's devotion and valor will forever live on.

*Portrait of a hero*

# K-9 Bear
# "Fur and Fangs"

Officer Bernie Greer knew dogs well. He had worked with a bloodhound named Bo that had found over two-hundred missing people. The dog had become old and slow and spent his senior years following the scent trail of rabbits when he was no longer able to go to work. He never did catch a rabbit, but Bernie knew he enjoyed trying. Seeing his old partner slow down in retirement, Officer Greer was ready for another dog. That dog was Bear.

*Retired bloodhound, Bo, meets Bernie's new dog, Bear.*

***Bear***

Unlike the laid back bloodhound, the new dog showed much enthusiasm and boundless energy. Bernie and Bear were on call to respond wherever needed in Orange County, Florida. Bear was unusually young when he joined the Police Department. He graduated from training when he was only one-year-old. As a result, he was not quite sure of himself before his first search. Very quickly, that night came.

Bernie and Bear were called to search a two-story home that had been burglarized. Bear was eager to respond, but he lacked the assurance an older more mature police dog would have had. Full of spirit and heart, Bear bounded up to the second floor of the home to look around. Everyone waited. When Bear did not return, Bernie became more concerned and suspicious that the burglar might still be in the home. Then he turned to see Bear standing in the doorway of a bedroom, hackles raised and growling ominously. The officer carefully approached the same doorway to investigate. When he slowly peeked in, he saw that Bear was looking into the children's bedroom. There sat a cardboard poster of a Jedi character from Star Wars. Bear did not like the frightening poster and would not go into the room, so Bernie went in alone. Relieved it was only a poster, Bernie tried to call Bear into the bedroom to reassure him.

"Come on, Bear," he called to the reluctant canine.

With much hesitation, Bear approached the doorway once more and peeked inside. When he was just half-way in, Bernie accidentally bumped the chair that held the poster causing the Jedi to tumble to the floor. It was as though the Jedi had come alive, and the dog scrambled and fled. He ran as fast as he could to the first floor of the house where he growled from the safety of the living room. The incident was amusing to everyone searching the home except Bear. No burglar was ever found.

As time passed, the dog eventually matured and became more experienced. He proved himself, repeatedly, to be a qualified addition to the police force. Before too long, he was involved in over thirty arrests.

One evening, Bear and Bernie responded to a break-in at a lawnmower dealership. The burglar had cut a hole in the side of a building and crawled inside. When Bear arrived, he immediately ran through the same hole to pursue the suspect. In the dark, Bear ran directly to the showroom where new lawnmowers were on display. In the grey shadows the burglar crouched quietly trying to conceal himself behind a lawnmower. The bright beam of Bernie's flashlight swept over the room. Like a small halo of sunlight illuminating the dark of night, it panned the blackness. Suddenly it stopped. A man cowering near the floor was caught in its brilliance. Bear was nose

***Bear in agility training***

***Recognition for a fine performance.***

to nose with the suspect bearing a fearsome expression only a police dog can muster for such an occasion. Bear had gotten his man.

After a long night and much excitement during his 7 p.m. to 5 a.m. shift, Bear returned home to enjoy his favorite treat, a piece of summer sausage. He settled down in his favorite sleeping place, the hallway between the bedrooms of both of Bernie's sons, and he fell into a much-deserved sleep. He would awaken later that day by 3 p.m. to wait at the door for the boys to return home from school.

From time to time Bear, as well as other police dogs, had to return his focus to re-training to keep his skills sharp.

One day when Bear was put through his paces, he was sent to attack the heavily-padded sleeve that is used to train K-9s to hold with their teeth. As another officer pretended to be a suspect, Bear charged after him with great vigor. He lunged at the padded arm and sunk his teeth deeply into the padding. But something was not right. When Bear released his hold on the padding, one of his upper canine teeth had broken off. He could have fared well with only one, but later in another training exercise, he broke the second of his intimidating long upper-canine teeth.

Bear's doctor explained that the dog had unusually long and narrow teeth for a German shepherd, which had caused the problem. Bernie and the veterinarian, who was also a dentist, knew that a police dog without teeth is like a police officer without his gun. The dog would have no protection, nor could he protect his officer. They discussed a solution for poor snaggle-toothed Bear.

It was decided that the veterinarian/dentist would fit Bear with a fine set of steel teeth. First, each tooth required that a root canal be done the same way it is done for humans. The procedure deadened the nerve to prevent further pain. Bear underwent two procedures two weeks apart. Two steel anchors were placed around the roots of the teeth. Then "spikes" were glued onto the anchors, and they were capped. For a few days, Bear ate soft food and took antibiotics. Then he was back on the job. Bear seemed quite pleased with his set of shiny steel teeth, and with a silvery flash of his teeth, he showed that he was ready for many more years of police service. The implants had saved his career. His jaws were once again capable of clamping down with more than the one thousand pounds of pressure he would need to perform his duties efficiently.

Many a fleeing suspect stopped in his tracks at the sight of Bear's forbidding dental work bearing down on him. Many a suspicious person stopped by Bernie changed his mind about giving the policeman any trouble after taking one look at Bear's gleaming teeth. Not only were the metal teeth durable against buttons, zippers or even a gun barrel, but they offered a fringe benefit of a most intimidating "smile." Bear was now an equal match to any burglar, robber or Jedi he would encounter.

Bear was used in the first FBI drug case where illegal drugs were tracked into the country to Orlando, Florida. A plane coming in from Puerto Rico landed at the airport there. It sat among a group of small planes near a hangar. Bear had trained on aircraft previously, but he had never searched a plane. With no air traffic to endanger the dog, Bernie got downwind of the planes and unsnapped Bear's leash and gave him the command to search. In less than a minute Bear found the correct plane and scratched on the door of the luggage compartment. A search warrant was obtained based solely on the dog's indication that drugs were on the plane. The search of the plane revealed several containers of illegal drugs. Bear was immediately rewarded by playing with his tennis ball. His success was instrumental in convincing the FBI of the usefulness of dogs in drug detection and searches as the illegal drug trade proliferated in Florida.

Bear served out his time with the department and retired. True to his grizzly name, he demonstrated strength and power and generated fear for those who opposed him. He was a dog with a razor-sharp smile never to be forgotten. But despite his frightening appearance and "strong as a steel trap" muzzle, K-9 Bear from the sunny State of Florida never once bit anyone.

*Jim and Ace*

# K-9 Ace
## "Jaws of Steel"

Officer Jim Bauerly sat on the floor in a room full of playful six-week-old German shepherd puppies and waited. Out of the litter, one playful pup ran right up to him tugging at Jim's pant leg with its soft little jaws. Ace was that puppy, and he won Jim over, finding himself a new home and eventually growing into a most handsome dog.

When Ace was still a baby, Jim began his training. He found that Ace had very strong jaws and a powerful retrieval instinct. Ace would bring to Jim anything he could find. Sometimes it was a ball, a Frisbee or a stick, but often he would grasp a heavy two-by-four in his mouth and with great effort drag it across the yard. Ace chomped and chewed and loved to wrap his teeth around anything he could get hold of, once even bringing a ball of thread no larger than a pencil eraser. Proudly, he spit it at Jim's feet.

Before long, Ace's play became serious business as he was thoroughly trained to do his job well. His strong holding instinct made him a fast learner when it came to holding a suspect.

"HOLD!" Jim commanded loudly.

Jim knew a good solid hold could save lives.

Ace learned he must not release his grip until told to do so. He became very skilled at holding with his strong mouth, and after training sessions he continued his bites and holds on his favorite toy, a black rubber brick.

51

***Ace on a rare occasion when his jaws were not clamped tightly shut.***

Ace's jaws were so strong he could clamp them tightly shut preventing Jim from opening the vice-like jaws to give the dog medicine. His ability to grip so firmly became legendary among K-9 officers and not one could pry his firmly-clenched teeth apart.

Ace thrilled to the sound of the car's siren. One day Jim turned on both siren and flashing red lights as he and Ace joined a high-speed chase. The police dispatcher's voice cut in and out on the radio as the siren wailed. Ace threw back his head and howled along. Jim picked up the car's radio microphone, and Ace's "singing" turned into loud barks. The jaws, normally clamped shut, were held wide open as he held his head back and continued his canine song.

"Ace!" Jim called to the noisy dog, ordering him to stop the racket.

But Ace was excited and would not stop barking. The Communication Center could not hear what Jim was saying, and he gave up trying to send his message.

Along eighty miles of highway and dirt roads and through four Iowa counties police cars sped as Ace howled. The suspect's car was in sight. Abruptly, the suspect screeched into a yard and bolted onto the back porch of a house ending the chase. Officers tore open their car doors and pursued the fleeing suspect. The officers were inside when Jim slammed on his brakes and jerked open his car door to join them.

From outside the house, Jim could hear two other officers inside struggling with the suspect.

"GET THE DOG!!" an officer yelled, and Jim assumed they meant Ace.

Jim and eager Ace rushed inside the house. Once inside, Ace was met by jaws more powerful than his own. A terrible snarling dogfight erupted as an angry pit bull charged him and sank its deadly teeth into Ace's shoulder. The small vicious dog held Ace in a painful grip determined not to let go. As the dogs grappled, Jim drew his gun. The pit bull released and tore into Ace again. Between the pit bull's snaps and Ace's yelps of pain Jim took aim at the small dog as it thrashed about. It was a moving target he would have to hit while simultaneously trying not to hit his own dog.

Jim maintained a careful aim.

CRACK!

Jim shot and wounded the pit bull.

Jim ran to Ace and carried the injured dog to the cruiser to race for medical help. After being treated for a gaping shoulder injury

**Keeping Iowa safe**

***Looking for a high-speed chase***

and after a period of recovery, Ace was soon back in the cruiser howling with the siren once again.

But far from the sirens and lights of a chase, on what seemed like a quiet night, an unforeseen danger lurked. On this night danger came quickly and unexpectedly. For six years, Jim had stopped at the Climbing Hill School to let Ace out of the car to take a break in the early morning hours. The dog usually ran behind the school and trotted right back to the car.

Jim stood alone outside the car on that quiet night waiting for nine-year-old Ace's return. When he did not return, the officer began to worry.

"Here, Ace!" he called to the dog.

Silence.

Jim grabbed his flashlight, its tawny beam slowly sweeping through the misted night and browned summer grass as he walked in the direction he had last seen Ace.

Suddenly Jim could smell sewer gas. He shone the yellowed light on an opening in the ground. A manhole cover had been removed, and the opening led to an underground septic tank that was twenty-five-feet deep and twelve-feet wide.

Jim hated to think what he might find down that deep tank. The eerie beam from his flashlight illuminated the dark hole and shone into two frightened eyes staring up at him.

Ace!

He could see the dog frantically clawing at the walls and swimming in the sewage. Jim ran back to his car and called for a rescue unit and then he drove his car directly to Ace's horrid underground prison. He shone the light down the hole again. Ace was tiring and becoming overcome by methane gas in the putrid tank. Soon it would render him unconscious, and he would slip below the surface for good. Only minutes remained to rescue Ace before the powerful gas would take his life. Jim knew Ace would never be able to last the time it would take for the rescue unit to drive eight miles to the school.

Just then Jim remembered a thirty-foot rope he had in the trunk of his cruiser. He jerked open the trunk, and his nervous hands found it. He tried to tie a loop of the half-inch wide rope to slip over the dog's head, but his hands were shaking too badly to do it. Instead, Jim lowered the long rope into the hole. Would Ace's famous jaws respond? Was he still able to understand commands?

"Take it!" Jim commanded the floundering dog, "TAKE IT!"

Increasingly weak, Ace valiantly reached for the dangling rope. With his last measure of strength the dog with the powerful jaws clamped down on the rope's end.

"HOLD! HOLD! HOLD!" shouted Jim down the dark hole in his familiar commanding tone.

And hold Ace did. As firmly as he would hold a fleeing felon, his jaws held tightly to the rope. Jim strained and pulled the taut rope dangling the ninety-five-pound dog up, up through the dark deep shaft to safety above.

Finally, Ace was safe above ground where he could breathe the crisp night air. He was so glad to be out of the hole that he ran to Jim to be loved. The fetid sewage clung to Ace's fur. Jim didn't care, and he embraced the very dirty dog. Jim had his dog back and that was all that mattered.

The relieved officer called a school official to open the building, and Ace was marched into the school gym for a shower. When the first shower didn't get the odor off, Ace was taken to a professional groomer the next day for a more thorough bath.

*Pleased to be once more above ground and clean.*

For nine years, the dog with jaws of steel served as a canine officer. When Ace was retired, Jim started working with a new dog, Andy, but still returned to get Ace on some nights after half a shift.

They stopped at "Mr. Donut," and Ace was then returned to his kennel to lick sweet icing from his paws. It was a fitting end to a career for a Sioux City, Iowa, dog that will always be the Woodbury County Sheriff's Department's Ace in the hole.

# K-9 Baron
## "Driven to Distraction"

Lt. Ron Schmutz spent twenty-five years working for the Allen County Sheriff's Department in Lima, Ohio. He trained his dogs well over those years and experienced both harrowing and routine days with them in all his years of service. As one of the most respected dog trainers in law enforcement, his career was a continual learning curve. Years of experience taught him the right and wrong way to do things, and in turn he passed along his knowledge to officers just starting out in police work. Over the years, his first dog, Baron, was both student and teacher.

Four-year-old Baron was well known to the department. Often during roll call, Ron brought Baron along. Once off leash, the black and tan German shepherd visited with all the other officers as they sat in their seats waiting for roll call to begin. Most played with him and petted him, but Ron knew he could get a rise out of a few of the less-canine oriented officers when he gave the dog a special command.

"Smile," he would say with a sparkle in his eye.

Dutifully, Baron pulled back his lips to display his sharp canine teeth. Much to the amusement of the others, Baron gave a low, menacing growl intimidating some of the men who squirmed nervously in their chairs. They did not fully understand that Baron was only playing and would never bite them.

Feeling very much at home during roll call, Baron wandered over to the water fountain. Standing tall on his back legs, he placed his front legs up on the wall-mounted fountain and then slid his left leg across to locate the button. Once he located it, the thirsty dog gave it a hard push so he could noisily slurp the cold water. His intelligence and good humor amused others and also made him an easy dog to train.

Baron was a dog who liked to exit the car through the open window.

"Load up" was his command to re-enter the car through that same window, and the sight of him responding to the command brought many smiles from spectators at K-9 demonstrations.

**Ron and Baron**

***Baron's favorite exit strategy***

Occasionally, Ron and Baron were called upon to transport suspects who did not normally ride in K-9 cars. He had complete trust that Baron wouldn't bite a suspect unless aggressively provoked. However, Baron was trained to bite in order to protect the police cruiser. Before Ron could put anyone he transported in the front seat, he had to close the sliding door in the grillwork that separated Baron who rode in the back seat. Once the apprehended was in the passenger seat, Ron gave that person a warning.

"I'm going to slide open this door, and since the dog is trained to protect me and the cruiser, you're gonna have to sit REAL still so he doesn't bite you."

Then he turned toward the back seat.

"Be nice," Ron commanded Baron, but in reality he knew the command was not really needed.

Then he slid the small door open.

At that, Baron thrust his head through the opening. Slowly, and with much curiosity, he edged his nose close to the suspect's face. Then he began to sniff. And he continued to sniff. Soon, he

***Baron watches Ron search a "suspect" in training.***

was licking the suspect's ear, and because of his friendly nature he continued to lick the nervous suspect all the way to the station where with great relief, the suspect exited the car.

One summer Sunday morning, Ron had just returned from church when a call came that he and Baron were needed. The day was already growing hot as Ron and Baron reported for duty.

An elderly husband and wife had returned from church to their rural home to find a strange truck nearby. Three men were brazenly loading up all the couple's household belongings into a pick up truck. Surprised by the return of the couple, one of the men hit the homeowner over the head with a rolling pin leaving him injured and bleeding profusely.

A neighbor returning from the same church saw the unfamiliar truck and the men and drove over to find out what was going on. One of the men threw a rock, smashing the man's windshield.

The assailant and the other two burglars fled to the truck and sped off. Seeing that the elderly man was being cared for and the Sheriff's Department had been called, the neighbor gave chase in his own vehicle.

A township policeman twelve miles away spotted both vehicles racing though his jurisdiction and turned on his lights and siren to join in the chase. With the officer bearing down on him, the driver of the pickup truck crashed, and the three men escaped and scattered into a massive undeveloped area at the edge of the road.

The trio had stolen several hand guns during the burglary making the men "presumed armed and dangerous." On what was predicted to be a scorching day, over twenty police officers and squad cars from several jurisdictions arrived to set up a perimeter around the large area of weeds, water, mud and trees. No matter which direction the suspects turned, someone would be in the right location to apprehend them when they were flushed out of the woods.

Ron and Baron rode for twenty-five miles to the scene of the truck crash. Ron had never seen such a difficult area to explore. It proved to be so difficult to track there that the two backup officers he brought with him were not physically able to keep up and both gladly returned to the perimeter. He and Baron were on their own. They traversed the rugged terrain with great difficulty.

Tracking on his leash, Baron picked up the scent of the men immediately. He pulled Ron deep into the weeds, as the officer struggled to carry his gun in one hand and grasp the leash in the other. For half an hour they tramped along through the thickets and brambles. Then they approached the rear of a house. Panting Baron tugged at the lead to pull Ron towards the backyard.

Emerging from the woods, Ron peered about but could see nothing. Then his eyes fell upon a small overturned fishing boat. Tall weeds grew like a natural barrier around it. It did not appear to have been moved in years. With much caution, Ron approached the boat. Just then, Baron began his low growl. This was not the "smile" posture used to amuse the officers at roll call. This was a confident and determined indication Ron knew very well that forecast discovery and danger.

"Come out with hands and arms showing or the dog is coming in!" Ron yelled.

Baron maintained his alert and watchful stance.

The boat was slowly lifted upward, and a nervous man emerged with his arms in the air.

"I'm coming out----please, please, keep the dog away---don't let 'im go!" he pleaded.

The man still carried two firearms in his waist band.

Ron ordered him on the ground, spread eagled.

"Sit-stay" he told Baron, and with the dog watching intently, Ron searched and handcuffed the man and removed the guns. Any movement by the suspect, and Baron would make his own apprehension, as trained, without command.

Squad cars sped to the location, and the police took the suspect into custody.

That left the other two accomplices yet to find.

Ron and Baron returned to the woods to the last place they had seen multiple foot prints in the mud. Given the command to track, Ron "cast" Baron in semi circles, and soon they were off again.

Traveling in another direction, Baron found the second suspect hiding behind some trees a mile and a half further on. Seeing the torso of the suspect, Ron ordered the hiding man out. But the man refused.

Several more attempts were made for the suspect to step out from behind the tree with hands in the air, or the dog would be sent. Having only high weeds and thick thorn bushes for cover, Ron feared for his safety and decided to send the dog.

"Stop him!" he commanded.

Ignoring the possibility that the man may have possessed a weapon, Baron charged forward and leapt upward with lightening speed. He bit the suspect's upper arm until the screaming man fell to the ground. Baron released immediately when commanded, and the suspect tried a quick kick to the dog. This was a mistake on his part as Baron made a second bite on the suspect's lower leg. He held on until Ron could make the arrest.

The man admitted to losing a firearm in water somewhere in the forbidding terrain, so he was unarmed. With Baron leading the way through the underbrush and jagged tree branches that blocked their way, Ron and the suspect trekked on for nearly a mile to reach a backup officer.

Ron radioed his success.

"I've got one, and we're heading north to a road."

The suspect was surrendered to the other officer, and as the sun reached its zenith in the cloudless sky, the track continued.

Both Ron and Baron were exhausted. The hot summer sun bore down on the cracked and parched soil, and fingers of sunlight filtered into the impenetrable overgrown forest floor, heavy with weeds and brambles, making each step nearly impossible. With one more suspect to be found, the trackers turned back to where they had come and pushed once again through the dense tangle of vines and leaves that thwarted every attempted step.

Clouds of mosquitoes, whining in the dense bushes and muddy pools of stagnant water emerged as the two stumbled along. Humming and biting with a vengeance, they presented yet one more hazard. But, despite the intensity of the heat and the biting insects, Ron was determined that if Baron could go on, he could too. He paused to transmit his position.

"We're currently going west," he notified dispatch.

They had already covered three or more miles that day, and the hunt seemed endless. As he struggled onward, Ron received a call from the backup officers saying the two suspects in custody told them the third man did not have a gun, but Ron could not know that for sure and remained vigilant. Baron's track took them across several streams where the over-heated dog paused briefly to lap up the often brackish water before continuing on.

Handlers are trained to always stay with the dog. Even when the handler might observe some suspicious stomped down weeds or other telling signs on the ground, and even though the dog might track away from those signs, the handler must maintain full faith and trust in the dog's confidence and abilities. Ron studied the ground as they went. Every so often he could see the suspect's footprints in mud or weeds, so he knew Baron was not leading him astray. Reading the signs on the ground, Ron could see a foot print in the mud, and it was so fresh that water was still rushing back into it. He knew they were quickly gaining on the suspect. As they broke free of the solid ground cover and tangles, Ron could see a patrol car over a mile ahead sitting on a bridge.

Different jurisdictions all had their own radio frequencies, and most of time there was no shared frequency. All radio transmissions had to be relayed by Ron's dispatch to the dispatch of another agency. Eight or nine different departments were helping maintain the huge perimeter. Ron strained to recognize the squad car on the bridge, but it was not familiar to him. He relied on his dispatcher to attempt to notify all the departments ultimately finding the correct agency to identify the car up on the bridge and pass along his limited but crucial transmissions.

Sheer determination drove Ron, and his instincts told him that eventually the third suspect would be located and apprehended if he persisted. With the radio battery continuing to weaken, he gave his directional updates every few minutes, as the trek through the prickly woods continued directly towards the squad car. The officer and the dog had too much work invested in the day, and Ron wasn't going to let the last suspect get away.

Baron continued straight towards the cruiser, closer and closer. An arrest was imminent. The hunt would soon be over, and the officer in the car would jump out to nab the fleeing suspect before he could pass under the bridge. But Baron did not stop at the bridge. He tracked right up to the bridge and then right under it. Ron could see the suspect's footprints in the mud, and they continued on just beneath the cruiser that sat atop the bridge.

With much frustration, Ron realized the man had gotten past the officer in his vehicle and was now out of the area of containment.

Baron panted heavily. His fur was matted with briars and debris. Dirty and dripping with sweat, Ron looked upward. There sat an officer in the car with the air conditioning running keeping himself cool in the heat of the day.

"Do you realize that this suspect just ran under this bridge right under your nose?" Ron shouted upward.

Ron's dispatcher, he learned later, had no direct way of contacting the officer in the car by radio, and the man's small department used another county's radio dispatcher for communication. The waiting officer never heard any of Ron's radio traffic so never heard Ron was on his way directly towards him. After holding the perimeter for several hours, the officer had simply let his guard down, and the suspect slipped away.

When the officer realized what had happened, his face turned many shades of red with embarrassment, and he apologized effusively. But Ron was too exhausted to even speak. He called for a unit to pick him up.

When the unit arrived, Ron looked like he had fought a war. His arms, legs and face were scratched and cut from the broken branches and thorn bushes he was dragged through. His uniform was tattered and torn, and his boots were ruined. Baron had cuts on his paw pads but had never slowed or showed any signs of fatigue on the track. With great relief, Ron and Baron slid into the air-conditioned vehicle that arrived to take them home. Baron, greatly fatigued, stretched across Ron's lap and fell asleep. The forced air in the car blew cool breezes upon the over-heated dog. It would be the dog's only fond memory of the torrid and trying day. But Ron had it worse. Days later, when the itch of mosquito bites began to ease, he was tormented with a new and angry rash of poison ivy that covered his entire body.

Ron was the consummate teacher taking away a lesson from every experience. Instead of showing anger at his fellow officer who allowed the suspect to slip away under the bridge, he knew the man had just learned a valuable lesson that would serve him well in the future and make him a better officer.

The escaped suspect was taken into custody four days later when he was found at his grandmother's home. Admittedly curious, Ron visited with the suspect at the jail.

"I'd run as far as I could and hide behind them trees," the man said, as he scratched at his arm. "Then I'd hear you and that dog again and take off runnin'."

Ron asked him to continue.

"I tried runnin' in the water and runnin' in circles, but then I seen you comin' again."

Nothing could throw his pursuers off the trail.

"I seen that squad car on the bridge and the officer jus' sittin' there in it," he continued. He never did once look my way, so I figured I could slip right by 'im," the man said.

With a tiny bit of self-righteous satisfaction and justification, Ron had to chuckle as he listened when he noticed the man was continually scratching as he spoke. He, too, was covered with a red bumpy rash.

Poison ivy played no favorites.

Far from their forbidding refuge, all three burglars pleaded guilty and were given long prison terms.

After such an agonizing trek in the woods, routine patrol would seem like a relief. Once again, duty called.

Ron was working the midnight shift making the routine rounds "rattling door knobs" at businesses to make sure everything was securely locked up. It was warm and humid that August when he eased his patrol car behind a large strip mall at three o'clock in the morning and stopped in the deserted area. Ron exited his car leaving Baron safely in the back seat.

On patrol, Ron always left the sliding door screen between the front and rear seats open so that if he called to or needed Baron for assistance, Baron was free to exit the car by jumping into the front seat and out the driver's window or the open door. Although Baron was trained to stay in the rear of the cruiser unless needed, there were certain times that Ron softened his stance on the matter and allowed him to ride up front in the passenger seat.

Ron walked the length of five or six doors checking each one before returning to his cruiser. Routinely, he pulled ahead a short distance and got out to repeat the procedure. To save a little time, and admittedly feeling lazy in the early morning hours, the tired officer bumped up the gear shift from drive to neutral so that when he returned to the car, all he had to do was tap down the lever once again to move forward.

Ron had checked several doors and had his hand on yet one more doorknob when he heard a most familiar sound.

"Ka-klunk"

Suddenly, a shiver ran through him. It was the sound his cruiser made when it shifted from neutral into drive. Had someone with theft on his mind been watching Ron? Had someone stealthily slipped behind the wheel and commandeered the vehicle in his absence? It would be a brave thief who would be bold enough to steal a K-9 car. Had the car malfunctioned in some way he wondered?

Ron felt as if an electric bolt was going right through him as his eyes focused on the car. His mind raced as he imagined the worst. Slowly, the car moved forward. Momentarily frozen where he stood, his eyes strained through the early morning darkness to see who was driving it as the engine hummed, and the car continued in a straight line down the road.

The car was still at idle speed and moving slowly as panicked Ron ran to catch it. His heart pounded, and he raced madly as he mentally prepared himself to physically apprehend the car thief.

It was with much horror that instantaneously he recognized the driver. Through the window he could see the silhouette of two pointy ears and a massive fur head behind the wheel. The furry driver was content to continue the leisurely early morning drive, totally oblivious of the danger ahead.

Ron lunged at the door handle and tore the door open. Two surprised brown canine eyes greeted him.

"Oh, no!!" was all Ron could say as he watched Baron, sitting upright and proud behind the steering wheel.

"Back! Back! Back!" commanded Ron to the driving dog.

Baron was to return to the back seat area in the cruiser on command.

However, the dog found some pleasure in this new position, and for reasons unknown, he decided he was staying right there behind the steering wheel.

With the skill of a stunt man, the breathless policeman slid onto the driver's seat of the moving car pushing driver, Baron, aside. When Ron hit the brakes, the car jolted to a sudden and complete stop. A telephone pole loomed just twenty-five feet dead straight ahead. The car was silent but for the panting of the previous driver and Ron's sighs of relief.

***Danger behind the wheel***
Courtesy of Carolyn Kramer and the Middletown, Ohio, Police Department

After composing himself for five minutes to comprehend what had just happened, his first thought was anger at his dog who could have caused a costly accident, but within seconds, he realized that the dog had done nothing wrong. From all his training, Ron knew that it is the handler's mistake and not the dog's when there is errant behavior on the dog's part. Ron had gotten into the bad habit of allowing Baron to ride up front in the car. He never dreamed the dog would imitate him shifting gears. One sharp smack of Baron's paw on the gear-shift lever was all it took for the dog to try out his driving skills.

As daylight broke, and all the businesses which had been checked and secured in the night prepared to open for business, the police cruiser headed for home with Ron at the wheel and a dog resigned to the fact his driving days were over riding in the back seat.

Due to Ron's quick action, the next day's daily newspaper would not read, "K-9 Drives and Crashes Sheriff's Patrol Car." And Officer

Ron Schmutz would forever have a valuable lesson to teach rookie K-9 handlers.

Unless a K-9 possessed a valid driver's license, at no time should he ever be permitted behind the wheel.

Ron continued to train police dogs for many years. In his heart he knew that no matter how many dogs a handler might work with, they all would be measured by the memories of the first. He had been blessed with a loyal, intelligent and friendly dog. Together they had enjoyed companionship and adventure, and together they had endured hardships. Time would bring more dogs, smart, agile and perhaps even one prone to drive, but in his mind and heart, Baron would always remain "first dog," and set the standard for all that followed.

*Ron with his award-winning "students"*

# K-9 Ponch
# "Canine Clown"

The public does not always see the playful side of police dogs. Ponch, of Miami, Florida, was a valued member of the Police Department and had a very playful side. He was the partner of Bill Martin who was offered the dog when Ponch was just six-months old. Bill went to visit him in a yard where the young dog played. As Bill watched, Ponch merrily rolled a ball around in the grass completely fascinated with his own ability to keep the sphere moving. He was far too young to be used for police service, but his playful nature was a joy to watch as he showed a real fascination with the round ball.

After four months, Bill and a dog trainer re-visited Ponch. He was still very playful, and the two men worked with him for an hour trying to get him to show enough aggression to bark at the trainer. Finally, Ponch barked—just one time. That was enough for Bill. They would become a team. Ponch was taken to K-9 school and graduated first in his class.

After graduation, Bill took Ponch home. The curious dog sauntered through the house taking a leisurely tour. He sniffed out a room that was used as an exercise and weight room and made it his own. Ponch's round dog bed was put there, and he was quite content settling in to join a retired police dog, Max, and to befriend Rebel, a second German shepherd that was a family pet. The new dog had his

**Bill and Ponch**

***Ponch on Marine patrol***

own room, German shepherd playmates and children up and down the street to play with.

Duty called, and the partners started working the hot humid daytime streets of south Florida. Down dingy alleys and up sparkling blue waterways Ponch and Bill patrolled. The stifling heat prevented Ponch from wearing the bulletproof vest some dogs wear, but luckily he never needed one. In the heat of the day, he floated along the cool inland waterways on a marine patrol with the ocean breeze riffling through his fur.

Back on land, he occasionally searched a visiting president's plane for explosives, and often visited with school children, both welcome diversions from routine street patrol.

Ponch was a dog that had worked hard on land and sea. The air remained the last frontier for the versatile dog. That day came but not in the way he had expected. On that day, Ponch could have used a parachute if he could have gotten one.

Bill was called to search a building that had sat empty for years and was often robbed of its pipes and fixtures to be sold for scrap. After searching the first two floors, Ponch climbed to the third floor. He noticed a long open window with a very low windowsill that sat almost on the floor. It was an unusual window opening like he had never seen before. There was no glass but only a worn screen that opened inward. The screen stood open.

Ponch was curious as he stared at it. Seeing a tree just outside, Ponch walked toward the window. Before Bill could stop the dog, he watched in horror as Ponch walked through the window thinking it was an opened screen door.

Like a movie scene played in slow motion, the alarming vision ran through Bill's mind. With great trepidation, he raced to the window and looked down. Ponch had already hit the cement below landing on his feet. The stunned dog tried to steady himself, and when he did, moments later he ran off.

Bill ran down three flights of stairs imagining the worst scenario. "Ponch! Ponch!" Bill called as he burst from the building.

Luckily, dazed Ponch had not gone far. The dog was rushed to a veterinarian who found that he had only bruised his chest.

After Ponch's three-story fall another police officer gave him an "airborne badge" that he proudly wore on his collar next to his police badge. All the school children he visited liked to see it.

Shortly after getting his "wings," Ponch actually became airborne. When the State Highway Patrol wanted to experiment with airlifting dogs, it was Bill and Ponch who were first to try it.

Since most dogs get agitated when they are suspended in the air and cannot see their own feet, they become hard to control. Not Ponch. Relaxed and resting comfortably in a harness and sling attached by a cable to Bill's harness, Ponch floated along peacefully, surveying the ground below as he looked down from high in the air over the alligator-infested Florida swamps. The fact that he flew

*Ponch wearing his specially-made sling*

*Bill and Ponch await take off.*

*Ponch is lowered out the helicopter's door.*

*Mission accomplished*

*Ponch returns to terra firma and enjoys a run with Bill.*

so well meant Ponch could be lowered into difficult and isolated locations cars couldn't take him, making him even more valuable to the department.

Besides flying, Ponch's favorite activities involved sports. Sometimes it was playing tug-of-war with the neighborhood children, but other times he joined the professionals.

When the Miami Dolphins and Miami Hurricanes football teams played in Miami, it was Ponch that often entertained at half time. He showed his team spirit by wearing the teams' jerseys as he patrolled the stadium, and he always switched team jerseys at the half.

It was at half time that playful Ponch really shined. While the fans cheered, Ponch, representing the offense, took to the field. He chased a pretend suspect, the defense, down the long green field with thousands of fans watching and cheering as loudly for the dog as they did for the football teams.

The performances were not without humor. Ponch gave all the fans a laugh during one particular rainy half time. As the pretend suspect ran down the wet field, Ponch charged after him. This time

*Waiting to get in the action*

the dog misjudged the distance to the running man and missed him entirely as he leapt upward for the tackle. Instead of bringing his man down, Ponch slid for five yards on his back after passing the suspect. He regained his footing and decorum and finally caught his man. As local television crews filmed, the crowd roared. Postgame it was a difference story. While the football players showered, Ponch, who had always hated water, refused to take a bath.

Each year Ponch joined the crowd at Miami's Orange Bowl for the yearly, "Pig Bowl" where the Florida police raise money for charities. Much of his off-duty time was spent in charity work.

When the Fellowship House, an organization that supports the mentally ill in Miami, needed to raise money, Ponch was called on once more. His friends at Fellowship House built him a special ramp from which to bowl.

Bill polished up Ponch's standard sixteen-pound bowling ball and dressed him in a colorful bowling shirt. At the bowling alley, Ponch was paired with humor columnist and author, Dave Barry, who wore a matching shirt. The public donated money for every pin Ponch knocked down. A local songwriter wrote a rap song about Bowling Ponch, and when the television network CNN heard it, they put the entertaining canine on the air for the whole nation to see.

When it was Ponch's turn to bowl, he stood up on his back legs and knocked the ball down the ramp with his teeth. As the ball rolled down the alley towards the pins, Ponch often barked and chased after it, his toenails clicking, once again showing his sliding skills, but this time on the shiny wooden floor. But he soon learned his ball would always come back, and he ran to the ball return tunnel and poked his furry head down the hole and barked as if to hurry it along. Like magic his ball returned, and Ponch tried for another strike. The dog never tired of rolling the ball down the alley. Often he had a higher bowling average than many of the humans in the tournament. In the past, he had been able to score as high as one hundred and twenty.

*Reminiscent of playing with a ball in puppyhood*

*Ponch modeling his bowling shirt*

*Ponch with opponent, author Dave Barry*

*Ready to bowl*

*Hoping for a strike*

*Watching the ball return*

Besides having a good time, Ponch earned much-needed money to help all his friends and supporters at Fellowship House.

But not all days were for play. As Bill and Ponch patrolled one hot night, dispatch sent out a call. Two suspicious men had been seen prowling around a vehicle in an apartment building parking lot. Bill was the first to respond and pulled into that parking lot which sat in the center interior of two buildings. He parked next to a yellow Volkswagen. Bill and Ponch exited their vehicle and started checking all the cars parked in the lot. As Bill started walking away from the car, Ponch showed particular interest in the Volkswagen. An anonymous caller, no doubt watching from one of the apartment windows, made another call. Dispatch relayed the message directing Bill to the yellow Volkswagen. He returned to the car and using the light from his own headlights to illuminate the dark parking lot, he shined his flashlight to light the interior of the car. The door was locked, but through the window, he could see keys dangling in the ignition. In the still of night, he could hear muffled cries coming from the trunk in the front of the car. As the cries became louder, Bill reached for the latch and popped open the trunk. Inside was an hysterical young woman who had been bound and gagged.

Bill quickly removed the gag, untied the woman and helped her out of the trunk. Barely able to speak, she explained that her car had been hijacked, and she had been abducted by two men and sexually assaulted in the parking lot. Then the men bound and gagged her, stuffed her into her car's trunk and quickly disappeared. Bill tried to calm her and called for back-up.

When a second unit arrived to care for the traumatized woman, Ponch and Bill started their search for the men. They did not have far to search. Approaching an overturned dumpster one-hundred and fifty yards from the car at the side of the apartment complex, Ponch immediately alerted. There was not a sound, but Ponch was sure of his find. In the shadows, Bill could see an arm sticking out from the side of the dumpster. Ponch barked loudly as Bill ordered the subject to come out where he could be seen. With that, two men emerged from the dumpster. Both were taken into custody and placed in a police vehicle. Upon further checking, two handguns, one revolver and a semi-automatic were found behind the dumpster and were removed as evidence. The men were in close shooting range and had watched every move Bill made.

The victim later identified the men and the weapons. At the police station, both men confessed to the abduction and assault. They admitted they were getting ready to shoot the woman through the trunk of the car when Bill and Ponch arrived. At that point, they fled to the dumpster to hide and wait. Their hope was that Bill and Ponch would not find anything and would leave. Then they would re-emerge from their hiding place and kill their victim. With great alarm, they watched as Bill opened the trunk and found the victim. Their new plan was to kill Bill and the victim, but they admitted it was Ponch that kept them from acting. They knew the reputation of police dogs and feared what might happen to them if they killed Ponch's partner and the dog turned on them. Two lives were spared that night. Both men were eventually convicted of armed abduction, sexual assault and using a firearm in the commission of a felony. Then they were locked away for good.

As Bill would say years later, Ponch was always there when he needed him and so many times the dog probably saved his life in instances when Bill was not even fully aware of the danger surrounding him.

On land, air and sea, Ponch was a K-9 who never let a criminal slip away. On the bowling alley his strikes proved him to be the mentally ill's best friend. And in the hidden, steamy back alleys of Miami, his strikes proved him to be the criminal's worst nightmare.

K-9 Ponch, whose personality would be well-suited to a circus, was proud and playful but always one-hundred per cent police.

# K-9 Argus
## "A Cry in the Dark"

At half past three in the afternoon, a disturbed woman walked into the maternity ward of a Canadian hospital. She knew exactly what she was looking for. Having feigned a pregnancy she believed would buoy a failing relationship with her recently-absent boyfriend, she decided to steal a baby.

*Kelowna General Hospital*

Posing as a photography student, the woman asked a new mother if she could borrow and photograph the mother's newborn baby boy. With the tiny helpless baby in her arms, the woman vanished from the hospital and met two young male accomplices she had recruited earlier by telling them that someone she knew in the Hell's Angels would pay handsomely for the right baby. Hoping to receive a lot of money, the young men put the baby in a red gym bag and fled the hospital by car along with the kidnapper.

From four to six o'clock the woman cared for the baby in her mobile home. But when media attention intensified, and the search heated up, she panicked. The woman frantically cut and dyed her hair but soon realized her efforts were futile. She must get rid of the baby. Twenty minutes later, a Canadian Mountie knocked at her door.

A fifteen-year-old boy, previously removed from his unstable home, came to visit his mother, the kidnapper, in the mobile home park. At six o'clock, he peered towards the adjoining woods and watched two teenage boys carry a bundle into the woods. The boy crept behind and watched as one of the boys took the bundle into a ravine and came back empty-handed. The curious son confronted one of the boys he had watched and asked what was in the bundle.

"A baby," the young man truthfully replied.

The son, greatly agitated, retuned to his grandfather, the kidnapper's father. The grandfather asked why he was so troubled, and the boy told the story of what he saw. The grandfather picked up the phone and called the police to leave an anonymous tip knowing he was implicating his own daughter. He said a baby had been abandoned near the "old trail" in the suburb of Westbank, near the local mobile home park. It was now 11:40 p.m.

Just after midnight, the first K-9 unit arrived at the scene. Cpl. Gerry Guiltenane parked his black Chevy Tahoe dog wagon near the woods. In the far back seat compartment rode K-9 #404, Argus, of the Royal Canadian Mounted Police.

*Gerry and Argus*

The dog was a member of the Royal Canadian Mounted Police Dog Services, the longest continuously-running police dog training program in North America. Argus had been recently retrained to search after two years of service in bomb detection at the Alberta Airport. He was a multi-talented dog who had earned his place in the prestigious department.

Gerry stepped out of the car into the black of night. The only thing he heard was the soft gurgle of running water tripping over stones in the ice-cold creek.

Gerry faced a dark triangle of wooded land three-quarters of a mile long by half-a-mile deep. With a bouncing flashlight beam illuminating the surrounding shadows, the dog searched the easiest terrain first moving briskly though the pastureland to the south. Branches brushed against dog and man, and broken twigs snapped underfoot as Argus scrambled through underbrush and brambles so thick that Gerry, who followed behind the unleashed dog, could not

***Isolated and inhospitable to a newborn***

see anything that resembled an "old trail." He wondered if they were heading the wrong way.

It was typically cold in British Columbia's Okanagan region that fateful night, and the temperature had dropped to a bone-chilling 41 degrees. Soon the Canadian wind would find its teeth. Wild predators roamed the thick woods in the Canadian wilderness. Only a week before, a cougar had been sighted in the vicinity where yapping coyotes were common and lumbering bear were occasionally seen. These thoughts were left unspoken but constantly on the minds of Gerry and Investigator Gary White, who accompanied Gerry and Argus. Dual beams from their heavy-duty flashlights cut though the darkness trying to keep up with the large German shepherd that trotted ahead.

It had been nearly ten hours since the two-day-old baby, Denver Giroux, had been stolen from the Kelowna General Hospital, and now in the early morning hours all that could be heard was the heavy breathing of the focused men and the crunch of their footsteps deep in the woods as they plodded along adjacent to the rippling creek. Police Service Dog, (P.S.D.) Jake, a Belgian malinois, arrived with his handler, Steve Scott, just as Argus finished searching the pasture. The dog masters decided to split the remaining northern region where McDougall Creek divided the desolate area. Tangles of thick brush and rough-hewn trees interwoven tightly together created a natural barrier that made access to the creek bed nearly impossible. By using the two Level Four dogs, the Royal Canadian Mounted Police utilized the most highly-trained dogs they had, but it was slow going to make progress through the rugged terrain. If the dogs failed to find the baby, a growing group of volunteers stood ready to search the area again. Time was growing short. It was like racing against an invisible hand that could reach inside to stop the pendulum of a grandfather's clock signaling time had run out.

While the search continued, the police pleaded with the kidnapping suspect at the mobile home park. She callously and steadfastly refused to help them as they pleaded for the baby's life.

In the woods, Gerry and Investigator White, both growing weary, finally climbed to the crest of a dark hill. Inch by slow inch, they felt their way down into the ravine trying to keep up with determined Argus. Then they spotted him up ahead.

Suddenly, the dog's demeanor changed. At 1:25 in the morning, Argus stopped abruptly just ten feet in front of the men. He cocked his large head inquisitively to one side and listened. Argus remained alert as he stood perfectly still in the cool night air taking everything in. Gerry knew Argus well. The dog's acutely sensitive ears had picked up something. He was a reliable and experienced dog who did not give false indications.

In the murky blackness of night the men and dog stood quietly at that spot and listened. The men dared not utter a sound. At first it was very faint, but there was distinctly a barely audible sound in the night. Like a small bird's call, the high-pitched cry in the distance broke the silence.

"Argus," called Gerry, excitedly, "search 'em out!"

Argus charged forward a full one-hundred feet ahead in his eager quest to follow up on his find. The Mounties struggled to keep up as Argus bounded through the woods. Soon they were all on an overgrown path. It was the "old trail" that had been described to the department by the tipster!

The cry grew louder and clearer. A cold and hungry baby sobbed in the night. Rays of bright light from both flashlights danced across bare tree branches and criss-crossed on the ground as the two men ran to catch up with the dog. The joint glow settled on Argus down in a gully, and in front of him was Denver Giroux. The dog stood at the baby's side just at the edge of McDougall Creek, hidden under, and

*The brush and weeds of McDougall Creek where the baby was found*

concealed on all sides by, brush and weeds. At 1:30 a.m., September 28, 1996, the search was over.

Wrapped in an old black and red lumberjack's shirt, the baby's tiny bare legs, exposed to the harsh elements, kicked as Argus tenderly nuzzled the soft skin with his cold nose. The baby's skin was extremely cold to the touch. White scooped up the helpless child, opened his jacket and shirt and tucked the frigid baby inside against his own warm skin to raise the infant's body temperature. Gerry took his radio from his duty belt. His voice crackled the joyful message to all those waiting to hear.

"P.S.D. Argus has found the baby. He is alive but very cold. We're trying to get him out of here now."

Tiny Denver Giroux was carried out of the woods to a waiting ambulance and returned to the hospital where he had been born only two days before. Hypothermia had begun to set in. Without the dedication of the Mounties and Argus, he would not have survived much longer. The successful find in the woods was the culmination of the most extensive police mobilization ever launched in Kelowna.

Argus was later given the "Hero Dog" award from the German shepherd Club of British Columbia. The grateful parents of the baby were effusive in their praise of the Canadian Mounties for their hard work. For the K-9 Mountie, they gave a special thank you. Denver's parents presented Argus with a blue leather collar with an engraved nametag which read simply, "Argus."

The name would not soon be forgotten by the family of Denver Giroux. The child would grow up to hear the story one day of how once on a cold Canadian night a dedicated four-legged Mountie searched deep in the woods and against all odds heard an endangered infant's desperate cry in the dark.

# K-9 Axel
## "The Hungarian Surprise"

A proud three-year-old dog arrived at a police dog kennel in Kansas. He was Schutzen trained in Hungary and sent to the United States to do police work. Schutzen is a German word that means protect. His training represented the most strict and intense method of training police dogs. This training made him extremely valuable, and many police departments could never afford a highly-skilled Schutzen-trained dog. In addition, this dog had unusually beautiful markings. A rich black coat covered his sleek body, and a dark mask of fur covered his large deep eyes. People who saw him were in awe of his beauty. Criminals would fear his ferocity.

When a trainer from Lemont, Illinois, saw Axel, he bought the gorgeous dog for $2500. With such beauty and intelligence the dog would surely be a welcome addition to the Lemont Police Department.

At Chicago's busy O'Hare Airport, Officer Jerry Lehmacher, who had been assigned the dog, met Axel's plane. The dog was nervous from being kept in his flight kennel, but Jerry's quiet words soothed him. Immediately, he showed affection to this stranger by nuzzling the unfamiliar hand in hopes of being petted.

Jerry had his first police dog. He showed off the stunning animal to everyone. For the first week and a half, Axel stayed home relaxing and getting to know Jerry and his wife, Laura. Then he started to train.

Because Axel was from Europe, he only understood German. For eight weeks of training Jerry spoke to him in his familiar language.

"SITZ!" Jerry ordered Axel, and the dog sat down.

He looked to Jerry for his next command

"BLIEB!" said Jerry, meaning stay.

Then, it came time to search a room.

"VORAN!" Jerry called.

Axel began his search. As he made his rounds, Jerry was pleased with his performance.

The dog's final training command was "PACHEN!" meaning attack. At that command, Axel easily chased a trainer wearing a padded sleeve.

By the time he graduated, Axel knew all his commands, never flinched at the sound of gunfire and had the best nose in the class for tracking.

When Axel saw Jerry's police uniform, he eagerly ran to the door to go to work and patrol the streets of Lemont. He loved his job, and he loved to ride in the car.

But as days went by, Jerry noticed that as they searched buildings, Axel was unsure of himself. He seemed to hesitate and wanted Jerry to point to the places he should search. At each turn, Axel stopped and turned to see if Jerry was behind him. Only then, would he go on. Where another police dog would charge ahead on his own searching an entire house, Axel took each room slowly and moved on only when Jerry was near. Not knowing what was around the next corner troubled him.

One night, two men ran from a stolen car, and a police car chased them. Jerry's car sped to the scene and was the second to arrive, screeching to an abrupt stop. With adrenalin pumping, Axel bounded out and chased the men to a garage where they took refuge.

Other police officers on patrol listened over their car radios and raced toward the garage where Axel had the men trapped. When they arrived, the cars surrounded the garage. Red and blue lights atop the cars flashed in alternating sequence, lighting up the dark sky. Car radios crackled out messages, and police officers ran and shouted.

Axel froze. He no longer cared about the men in the building. His furry head darted nervously from side to side as he watched all the excitement. Then he began to pace. With a tremendous tug of his leash, Axel jerked Jerry along as the dog tried to run away from the scene. Axel wanted to get as far away from the action as he could. Jerry tried to collar correct him.

"NO!" he yelled as he gave a quick jerk on Axel's collar.

Axel still pulled away to run.

"SITZ!" Jerry corrected again, using the familiar German command.

But uncharacteristically, Axel refused to sit. As the men in the garage surrendered, Jerry allowed frightened but relieved Axel back in the car. The fearful dark eyes peered at Jerry in the car's rearview mirror as they drove away. Tracking criminals no longer appealed to Axel.

The police department had spent so much money on Axel that they decided to try him at drug detection. With high hopes, they paid another $2500 to send Axel back to school.

At first, Axel did well with his training. Each time he found marijuana wrapped in a towel he learned Jerry would stop and play with him. Then the detection got harder. Small bags of drugs were hidden in one of six empty cardboard boxes that were stacked against a wall.

Jerry slapped his hand on a table.

"SOOK!" he called, giving the German pronunciation of the search command.

But Axel did not want to seek.

The sharp slap of Jerry's hand on the desk startled Axel. He bolted from the room and hid. Jerry followed after him and spoke gently to him and coaxed him back. Time after time, the sound of the noise scared him, and he ran. Slowly, Jerry taught him to find the drugs in the boxes. When Axel finally found the drugs, he hesitated and reluctantly pawed at the box.

With a thundering crash, some of the stacked boxes tumbled down.

Axel was terrified. He once again ran. Patiently, Jerry reassured him. He tried more familiar training with the padded sleeve to calm the dog.

"PACHEN!" Jerry called, but Axel was too nervous to attack.

Jerry got behind the dog and gently pushed him towards the training sleeve. Axel grabbed it. Just then, the timid dog bumped into the boxes, and they began to fall. Axel released his bite, which a police dog should never do until told.

It was no use. Axel could not concentrate on his job. After three

weeks of training, the trainer pulled Jerry aside.

"He's not going to make it," he said, knowingly.

Jerry knew that if Axel could not concentrate on his work as he tracked burglars and robbers, he would put the lives of the other police officers in danger. And now drug detection training had failed.

***After leaving drug-training classes, Axel's options became much more limited.***

With much regret, Jerry and Axel returned home. On the way home, Axel nuzzled Jerry's hand to be petted just as he had done the day they met.

Axel had lived with Jerry for eight months, and Jerry had grown to love the dog. Axel's police career was over, and the dog seemed to sense it. Hard decisions had to be made about Axel's future.

The dog's deep brown eyes searched their faces as Jerry and Laura spoke of him. Since he came with a guarantee from Hungary

**Frightened and reluctant to do police work, the tables turned, and Axel looked to Jerry to protect him.**

that said he could be exchanged if he did not work out, Axel could be returned. Another dog would be sent in his place. Axel would be re-trained to break his bad habits. Jerry knew the re-training would be hard on the dog. It could possibly break his spirit. His personality would never be the same. If Axel could not be re-trained, he would be of no use to police departments, and the trainers in Hungary would most likely have him put down.

Through long discussions and tears, the decision was made. Axel had spent too many nights wedging himself between Jerry and Laura in bed as he settled in for a good rest. Jerry could not forget Axel's constant nuzzling for attention. Even now, he rested a paw in Jerry's lap. Jerry and Laura knew that they could never send Axel back to Hungary. Jerry took out his credit card and paid the police department $2500 for Axel. Despite the years of intense training, more than most dogs ever get, Axel had become a simple, but very expensive house pet.

When the newspapers and television reporters learned what had happened, they published Axel's story. Soon letters from all over the country arrived addressed to Jerry and Axel. Over $1800 was sent by total strangers to help pay for Axel.

All bought and paid for, Axel adjusted to his change of positions. He spent his days staying home and protecting Jerry's house. As a sideline, Axel faithfully watched over the family's twenty-pound cat, Boo-Boo. For Axel, it was the perfect low stress job.

Each day as Jerry left for work, he explained to Axel why he could not go. A new dog, Baron, took Axel's place in the car. The dog became Axel's best playmate. When Baron was off duty, Axel's

*Axel and Boo-Boo*

favorite game was to sneak up behind him and gently nip his back leg. Just as in drug training, Axel then ran to another room to hide.

***Jerry and Baron, Axel's able replacement***

When the Lehmacher family with its collective one-hundred-sixty pounds of German shepherds settled down for the night, it was Axel who slept on the floor next to Jerry, and Baron guarded the foot of the bed. Axel would guard the side of the bed into his old age when he passed away at the age of twelve after many happy years as a contented house pet.

***Axel and Baron***

When asked if he would do it all again, Jerry replied, "I'd pay double for him."

Just as not all people are suited to all kinds of work, K-9 Axel proved the same is true for dogs. He was the reluctant cop, from Lemont, Illinois, who turned out to be all beauty but no beast.

# K-9 Luke II
## "In Grateful Service"

It is hard to say how long he had been on the streets. He was small for his breed and did not exhibit the graceful slant back of a typical German shepherd. He ran loose on the streets on worn paws, scared and alone, fending for himself and scrounging food where he could find it. With no home, the raggedy dog found shelter where he could. During bad weather and in the evening, he hunted for a place to sleep and to wait out the long lonely nights. He was a housebroken dog, and he had been taught to sit and lie down. He was playful, intelligent and well-mannered having been someone's pet, but now he was separated from that owner and had to learn the ways of the often mean streets.

Worst of all, no one wanted him. He was a young dog, but in the relatively brief time he had lived, his days had already been hard as he roamed aimlessly on Ohio's streets and highways. Not even two-years old, he carried a piece of buckshot in his back left side no doubt inflicted by someone trying to scare him off when he was looking for a meal. The dog had become a furry hobo, bereft and with few options.

One day the stray was picked up by Butler County Ohio's Animal Control and delivered to the shelter in Trenton, Ohio. He was fed and had a roof over his head for the first time in a long time, but it was not a home.

Memories of a former owner had long since faded, supplanted by the harrowing ordeals of daily survival, and now he found himself in a strange and noisy place beyond his comprehension where he relinquished all control of his destiny. His stray companions demonstrated their own confusion in a constant chorus of barking like he had never heard before. After three days, by law, he could be put down, but sympathetic shelter workers deemed him adoptable

***Finally off the streets, the nameless dog peers sadly from his cage.***

and along with many other adoptable dogs decided to hold him as long as possible. They called the closest police department and offered the dog, but the department did not need a dog at that time, so the stray dog's future was uncertain, but decidedly looking much dimmer.

Sgt. Dan Nickum, working Vice Control, patrolled the streets of Cincinnati during the dangerous hours between 8 p.m. and 4 a.m. when a dog provided him much protection. He had worked successfully with a dog for a year and a half, but the dog ultimately developed health problems and was retired from the force leaving Dan without that companionship and protection. He would have to train a new dog.

Not long afterward, Dan went through three dogs in seven weeks at K-9 school. Two could not pass the veterinarian's exam, and the third refused to bite at the sleeve. Only seven weeks remained of the fourteen-week class he had started with them, and now he was desperate for a dog.

Dan's fellow officer, Ed Farris, worked successfully with a dog donated by an animal shelter and convinced Dan to consider a shelter dog. Calls from the department went out to all the local animal shelters. The only place having a German shepherd then was the over-crowded Animal Friends Humane Society of Butler County shelter. Scores of dogs arrived daily, and accommodations were stretched to the limit. The dog had been held beyond what he normally would have been the shelter employee said. Although he did not know it, the stray was due to be put down that day. Undernourished and perhaps a victim of false hope, still the nameless dog peered from his cage and patiently waited.

Dan and Ed paid the shelter a visit and amidst a chorus of constant loud barks were led to the stray dog's cage. Despite his hardships, the dog was playful when he saw the officers approach. Maybe he was too playful for police training. The dog's overly-friendly demeanor could mean he would not be able to muster enough aggression when it was needed on the job. And the dog's past experiences had taken their toll. His body was slight, still evidencing his days on the streets. His front legs seemed to be configured wrong, positioned too close to the back legs giving him an odd stance and not the typical sleek conformation that met German shepherd standards. Dan thought he looked more like a weasel. After much thought, and still skeptical, Dan decided not to take the risk, and the dog was returned to his cage.

But Ed intervened, and he suggested they take the dog off the shelter grounds to more accurately assess him. It was only then that the dog showed his other side. He was very driven to chase a ball, and Dan got him to bite a sleeve, which the willing "weasel" bit as though he had been trained to do it. He could be aggressive playing tug-of-war and seemed to be a quick learner. But he had one more hurdle to overcome. His hips needed to be checked by a veterinarian. Bad hips would wash him out of the program before he ever began. When his hips checked out alright, his chances of survival increased. The veterinarian judged his age to be about fourteen months. The buckshot in his lean side did not bother him and did not need to be removed, and his small frame would fill out nicely when he was properly fed.

With some reservations, Dan decided to take a chance on him. The shelter donated the dog, and after his dog license fee of $10.75 was paid, he wagged his tail and trotted out with Dan. Joyous shelter workers tearfully bid him farewell and wished him well. He was given a new name, Luke II, after Dan's first dog, Luke, and a career in law enforcement awaited the thin scruffy dog.

First stop on the way to his new home was at a McDonald's where the two shared some French fries, a first step in creating a bond. Luke II was taken to Dan's home to join his wife and four children, and after meeting them he got his first bath there. Then, starting far

*Dan and Luke II*

behind the other dogs, he was enrolled in classes with the six other dogs that had such a big head start on him. Those dogs had already been trained to track and perform building searches. It was all new to him. There was a lot of catching up to do. So much was riding on the dog's performance. If he did not work out, he would be returned to the shelter where once again, his days would be numbered.

But Luke was a willing student and learned his lessons well. Dan had trained many dogs, and with his patience, expertise and confidence in the dog, they moved through all the lessons in record time. Dan could throw a penny into a field and command "seek," and Luke would find it and bring it to him. When told to, he would then spit it into Dan's hand.

The dog had a natural ability to leap. When confronted with a fence, he needed no running start. One leap from a standing position close to the fence took Luke up and over with ease.

"It was as though he had springs on his feet," said Dan.

Soon, Luke had mastered all phases of training and worked like a pro. In no time at all he caught up with his classmates and earned his diploma.

"He was like a light switch," Dan said of Luke and his obedience. He could attack a fleeing suspect, but the instant I told him 'leave it,' he backed off. If I told him everything was alright and ordered the dog to then kiss the suspect, he would."

It had taken a year of puppy food until Luke filled out nicely. His coat was shiny, his eyes were bright, and his former awkward stance disappeared. He began to look like the noble German shepherd he was.

Like the other dogs, Luke learned not to take food from anyone but Dan, so he would not risk being poisoned. If he found something on the ground by himself, he might put it in his mouth to taste it, but he knew he would have to wait for approval before going further. It was a totally different behavior than he had known on the streets as

*The shelter dog learned his lessons well.*

**This Certifies That**

8482
Badge Number

8/23/93
Date of Issue

Police Chief

LUKE II
Name

Whose Photograph Appears Hereon is a Member of the
**CINCINNATI POLICE DIVISION**

***Proudly police***

a food-scavenging stray when the smallest morsel would be eagerly pounced on and devoured.

Both dog and man knew the streets well. Together they responded to burglar alarms, shots fired, robberies, traffic stops for drug detection and assaults.

Whenever called, they conducted tracks searching for whatever needed to be found. In the day-to-day police world, some calls were routine and non-threatening, and some calls were far more ominous.

After just six months on the street together, a call came for Dan and Luke to respond to an area where a drive-through had just been robbed. The robbers had forced the clerk down on his knees and then took approximately one-hundred dollars from the cash register. As the frightened clerk pleaded for his life and begged them not to shoot him, they fired a fatal shot and fled.

Immediately, three police departments responded, and the drive-through was surrounded by their cars. But the assailants had fled on foot. And although the robbery took place in Cincinnati, they had fled into another close-by township. That gave the township dog priority in tracking them. He was attempting to pick up the track when Dan and Luke arrived. For whatever the reason, the first and more-experienced dog was having trouble picking up the track. It was thought perhaps the suspects had fled in different directions. No one knew for sure.

Dan got Luke from the car and hooked him up to his tracking harness. They walked to a grassy area, and Dan cast him out and told him to track. Alert and excited, Luke immediately picked up the track. Up a hill he ran and eagerly continued on across a field. He led Dan through several back yards and suddenly stopped at the rear door of a residence. Dan pulled him away and cast him out again to make sure the track really stopped at that location. Once again, Luke returned to the same spot. He immediately started scratching at the door.

Dan called for the other officers who knocked on the door and found the suspects inside. Luke and Dan waited by the back door in case the suspects decided to flee. They did not. Luke's presence was a strong deterrent. The arresting officers found the stolen money inside a shoe and more in a closet, and the suspects had no choice but to surrender.

It had taken Luke less than ten minutes to find them. His find meant the pair would later be convicted of armed robbery and homicide and locked away where they could no longer harm anyone. The majority of K-9 officers could finish their entire career and never apprehend a homicide suspect. Luke had once been the hunted himself, and now he was the hunter. The $10.75 dog had just found two homicide suspects and reinforced all the confidence placed in him. He had proved his worth in a big way to the public he now protected.

But Luke was just hitting his stride. He loved going to work. His internal clock told him when it was time. At the same time before each nightly shift, he nudged Dan to get ready. Then he sat by the back door waiting, often not so patiently, wiggling about in eager anticipation. If Dan was too slow, Luke raced through the house to find him and barked excitedly to speed up the process. Then to Luke's satisfaction, they would go out into the perilous night to patrol and see what awaited them. It was never a long wait.

The early morning hours brought out many nocturnal creatures both two-legged and four-legged. Luke developed a great interest in raccoons as he patrolled outside the car and caught a fair share of them. A battle with feisty ground hogs once caused a trip to the veterinarian's office, and Luke strutted out with a shaved neck and forty-four stitches. His favorite toy was a soft sheep-skin animal, but unlike that peaceful creature he learned the hard way that live ground hogs and other creatures of the night did more than squeak.

In the early morning hours as most of Cincinnati slept, a man with less than lawful intentions crept through the police impound lot where many cars were stored. In the murky shadows, he searched for anything to steal from the cars that could be sold on the street for drugs and alcohol. Suddenly, a burglar alarm blared that warm summer night, and the startled prowler scrambled for a place to hide. Luke and Dan got the call and sped to the lot where Luke was released among the rows of cars to begin a search. In the thick darkness, Luke quickly disappeared down an aisle of cars and was out of sight. Dan tried to keep up and follow, and soon he heard a scuffle up ahead. When he caught up with Luke, he directed the bright beam of his flashlight until it captured just what he thought he would find. Hiding under a pick-up truck, a man fought to struggle free from Luke's clamped teeth.

*A force to be reckoned with*

Luke held the man as he thrashed, and the dog tugged at him forcefully, gradually jerking him out from under the truck.

"Leave it!" Dan commanded, when Luke had pulled the man out, and the dog immediately released his hold.

Then something fell from Luke's mouth.

Dan put the man in handcuffs, and then he shined his light on the object.

A pork chop!

"That's a real smart dog," the man said, "I brought them pork chops jus' in case a dog was here, so he'd eat 'em and not find me," he said.

Searching for the "bad guy," Luke had, indeed, found the pork chops. He picked one up to enjoy the taste, but remembering his training, he knew he would not be allowed to eat it. He had held the pork chop in his mouth as he tugged the man loose, and when he released the man, he also spit out the pork chop. The smell of meat had not deterred him from finding his man, and the brief struggle had afforded him the bonus of a taste of pork.

Dan and Luke returned home to sleep. At 4:30 a.m., Luke slipped quietly to his place beside the bed. It had been a good night.

Luke's job of protecting Dan never stopped. Just as the rest of the city was starting to awake, Dan and Luke were in a deep slumber. As Dan's wife arose and readied herself for work, she knew better than to leave the bedroom before she was completely ready. Once out the bedroom door, Luke would not let her back in. More than once, she had to yell through the door for Dan to wake up, so that she could get past Luke to be readmitted. The dog's loyalty ran very deep.

Luke was surely not the most expensive dog that ever became a K-9. He was not even the most handsome. But his heart was filled with gratefulness to the man who saved his life, and if put in a perilous situation, he would have gladly given his own life in deep gratitude. He was a "rescued dog," plain and simple—a $10.75 pound-hound bargain, who would never find his original owner.

But with his newly-found companion, the mean streets he had known became more bearable, and now he traversed them proudly and with self-assurance. To the Cincinnati Police Department, he was worth his weight in gold.

*The best companion $10.75 could buy*

***Dan and Midge***

Courtesy of John Hoffart, John's Photography

# K-9 Midge
## "Pint-Sized Power"

A reporter covering the Geauga County Sheriff's Office in Chardon, Ohio, faced Sheriff Dan McClelland who held a small dog in his hand.

"WHAT is that?" she asked.

Dan was used to such questions. When he introduced the new member of the K-9 team to his deputies, one looked skeptical, and in total silence he just stared.

"Pretty small," he finally said.

When Dan entered the office, he was holding one of the smallest dogs the K-9 officers had ever seen.

The dog was the runt of a litter whose father was a Chihuahua and whose mother was a Rat Terrier. The little dog could fit in Dan's hand. When Dan's daughter was growing up, she played with Barbie dolls, and Dan remembered the doll had a little friend named Midge. Now the dog had a name.

Dan had been looking for a small dog, but not necessarily one as small as Midge. He wanted to train a small dog to find narcotics in confined spaces. Since motor vehicles were often difficult for a large-breed dog to search thoroughly, Midge seemed the ideal solution. Often, when the larger dogs enthusiastically searched a vehicle, they damaged the car. If no drugs were found, law enforcement had to pay for the damages.

But as novel as the idea was, Dan had his doubts about this particular dog. One of his employees suggested the dog to him when the litter was born. Midge was the only dog not taken. She weighed only two pounds at ten-weeks old. At the employee's constant urging, Dan reluctantly agreed to meet the dog.

Two things immediately impressed him about the tiny dog. She was uncharacteristically calm around people, not always the norm for little dogs, and secondly, she was constantly using her nose to sniff everything. He was a man more accustomed to large German shepherds, but this was a dog he could scoop up instead of lead. He decided to give her a chance.

Each day, Dan took the small bundle to work with him in the police car to socialize her and to create a tight bond between himself and the dog. Up in the passenger seat sat petite Midge. Heavy screens on the rear door windows were installed for ventilation in the summer and to keep anyone from reaching in to take her, a consideration the handlers of big dogs did not have to worry about.

When a tight bond was established between Dan and Midge, she began to train. For the most part, she trained away from the big dogs. Her training was nearly identical to the large German shepherds with very few exceptions. If a large dog needed discipline, the correction was a slight jerk on the leash. But Midge was too small for such a correction. She was disciplined with a stern and loud, "NO!" That was all it took.

Midge proved to be so obedient that working off the lead was second nature to her. She learned to follow Dan from three to four feet away, so it was not possible for him to step on her. With her small size, he had to impress on her the necessity of returning to him immediately no matter what she was doing. Despite her police training, she was too easy a target for cars or strange dogs.

Midge was only three-and-a-half months old when she started narcotics training although German shepherds were normally eight-to-ten-months-old before they started. She would have a lot to prove to Dan and to the Sheriff's Department.

At first, Dan tucked marijuana in a small canvass envelope just four inches square. Then he began to play with Midge. She quickly made the association between the bag and the word "dope." Very briefly, he would play tug or fetch with the bag and the dog. Before she lost interest in the game, he put the bag away leaving her wanting to play more, thus building her drive to search for it. After a few days, Dan had someone hold her, and while she watched, he put the bag five feet from her around the corner of a desk. Midge was then set on the floor, and when she retrieved the bag, she received lots of praise and the reward of playing tug and fetch with it again. After much repetition, Dan began to hide the bag in harder to find places. When she became proficient, he took Midge to train in more congested places where she had to block out all distractions.

"Find the dope!" Dan called to her over and over, and Midge was off, returning proudly with the bag.

To alert Dan to her find, she thrust her small nose as close as she could to the drugs and then stopped what she was doing. With each find, she turned her head toward him and stared. Like a dog waiting for its owner to retrieve a toy just out of its reach, Midge's eyes communicated the need for Dan to intervene and help her with the rest of the task.

By six months of age she was accomplished enough to search school lockers.

*Midge quickly became an expert at locker searches.*

Courtesy of Laura Vokoun, Special Service
Deputy, Geauga County Sheriff's Office

While the shepherds normally took their Ohio Certification Test at age two, Midge took and passed the test when she was just one. That certification meant that the sheriff and his deputies could make an arrest, get a search warrant or seize property based solely on Midge's alert to the presence of marijuana.

Not everyone appreciated Midge's role in police work. Some people did not want to take her seriously at first, and some believed her presence on the force was an insult to the bigger traditional dogs. Dan's deputies were teased by other police departments, and his handlers were concerned that he would make them all carry little "Paris Hilton dogs," but despite all the good-natured ribbing, the deputies accepted Midge, and their dogs came to accept her too.

Most of the bigger dogs played with Midge in their off time, but one-hundred and twenty-five pound K-9 Brutus, who did not get along with the other German shepherds, liked her the most.

They saw each other daily in the office and soon formed a close bond. The unlikely "odd couple" was often found together, with Midge pulling at Brutus's whiskers or licking his nose. When their play was over, Midge curled up and nestled against Brutus's warm fur for a nap.

***Geauga County's odd couple, Brutus and Midge***

Courtesy of Laura Vokoun, Special Service
Deputy, Geauga County Sheriff's Office

*Even when playing with K-9, Ben, Midge holds her own.*

Courtesy of Laura Vokoun, Special Service
Deputy, Geauga County Sheriff's Office

***Always looking for fun with the big boys--Midge and K-9 Marco***

Courtesy of Laura Vokoun, Special Service
Deputy, Geauga County Sheriff's Office

It was a given that with her miniature size Midge would never do crowd control or perform other aggressive tasks. She found her own specialized niche, and that niche would remain narcotics detection. The passage of time soon gained her the respect of those who initially doubted her. At just fifteen-months-old, when the bigger dogs were just taking the certification test, little Midge had already found evidence of the presence of marijuana from the previous day in a school locker. It was confirmed by the boy's admission to a school official that he had placed it there. Midge later assisted narcotic agents with the search of a residence, and her skills were so refined that she successfully alerted to the location of marijuana and identified the location in the house where it had been smoked or used.

# CERTIFICATE

**The smallest police dog is
Midge
who measures 11in tall, 23in long,
and who works as an official
Law Enforcement Work Dog
with her owner,
Sheriff Dan McClelland (USA),
at Geauga County Sheriff's Office,
Chardon, Ohio, USA**

GUINNESS WORLD RECORDS LTD

*Midge holds the title of the World's Smallest Police Dog
according to the Guinness Book of World Records.*

Courtesy of Laura Vokoun, Special Service
Deputy, Geauga County Sheriff's Office

***Dan and his wife, Bev, pose with Midge who is
wearing her "Doggles" eye protection.***

Frequently Dan and Midge visited the local county jail to do narcotic searches, mainly of inmate property confiscated when the men were booked into the jail. The most hardened inmates softened when they saw Midge, and many asked to hold her. It was not unusual to see Midge cradled in the massive tattooed arms of some of the jail's hard-core felons. The prisoners knew her name, and her visits encouraged the prisoners to tell Dan about their own dogs and how much they missed them. The better an inmate behaved, the more he was allowed to interact with Midge as a reward. It was her own unique version of crowd control.

When Midge visited schools, all the children wanted to hold her and pet her. It provided the opportunity for Dan to explain to them that they don't have to be the biggest kid to achieve their own greatness, and even the smallest ones could often contribute in a big way.

***Good things often come in small packages.***

Courtesy of John Hoffart, John's Photography

Dan once received a letter from a mother of a student who attended a special needs class for children with learning disabilities. Her son was quite miserable at school when other children teased him and made fun of him for being pulled out of his regular classroom for the class. But when Dan took Midge to the special class for a visit, the young boy got to hold and pet the special petite member of the police force. After he returned to his normal classroom, all the children took interest in him and wanted to hear about his experience, and they wished that they, too, had gotten the same opportunity. From that day on, the boy did not mind going to his class, for it was there that he found out the class could be special in many ways, and he would always have the memory of meeting Midge there.

Being so small, Midge should live to be between eighteen and twenty-years of age, which would probably mean she could work until she turns at least fifteen.

Little Midge, who could once fit inside a teacup, has grown not only in size but in stature and has proved her worth many times over. She is one efficient and accomplished little bundle of law enforcement, highly prized by the department. And as long as she works, she'll never have a problem keeping up with the big boys.

# K-9 Sirius
## "New York's Shining Star"

The brightest star in the sky is the Dog Star, located in the constellation Canis (Dog) Major. The star is called Sirius, meaning "scorching." It is twice the size of the sun and twenty times more luminous. In Greek mythology it is believed to be the bright sparkling diamond in Canis Major's collar. In that constellation, Sirius is said to be crouching and ready to pounce. It is the star that accompanies Orion on his journey across the heavens. One dog in New York, the star's namesake, once shone briefly but just as brightly as he accompanied his officer on a day of tragic destiny.

Officer Dave Lim, an officer with the New York Port Authority, accepted the yellow Labrador retriever, Sirius, for his K-9 partner.

The animal, who was also the family pet when he was off-duty, soon grew into a one-hundred-pound dog that was, like the star, both notably brilliant and unusually large.

Sirius was a bomb detection dog at the World Trade Center in New York, and every day his powerful sense of smell ensured that the two stately buildings were safe for the thousands of people who worked within them.

One day when President Bill Clinton visited the area, Dave and Sirius helped to secure the heliport near the World Trade Center. The President came over to pet Sirius, and a White House photographer took a picture to send to Dave.

**Dave and Sirius**

*Off-duty Sirius rests in the sun.*

***Sirius receives a presidential pat.***

Courtesy of the White House Press Office

Dave and Sirius were seen daily at the World Trade Center buildings where they checked vehicles and packages for explosives at the loading dock. Employees in the two tall buildings that graced the Manhattan skyline smiled when they saw the familiar pair patrolling the area, and the sight of friendly Sirius on patrol made the dog's admirers feel safe.

But on one particular day, they were not safe. Under a sunny and cloudless blue sky, the morning of September 11, 2001, Dave and Sirius reported to the Port Authority Police Station, which was in the basement of the World Trade Center's Tower #2.

Suddenly, they heard a loud explosion, and Dave thought a bomb had gone off.

"One must have gotten by us," said an alarmed Dave, wondering how a bomb could have possibly gotten into either building.

He needed to investigate, and if a bomb had really gone off, he knew he would need two free hands to be able to help anyone who needed him. So before he left, Dave put Sirius inside his large kennel in the basement of Tower #2 to make sure the dog stayed safe.

"I'll be back to get you," he promised the dog, and Sirius's knowing brown eyes told Dave the dog knew it to be true.

Sirius settled down in his kennel with his usual contented, "O.K., I'll be here when you get back" facial expression.

Then Dave rushed off to help with the rescue effort in Tower #1.

When he came up from the basement of Tower #1, Dave could not believe his eyes. He could hear screams up through the stairwell, and he could see clouds of black smoke. The stairway was smoky, and Dave tried his best to direct people out. When he reached what he thought was the forty-fourth floor, he heard a second explosion which came from about the eightieth floor of Tower #2. From where he stood in the B stairwell of Tower #1, he felt the massive explosion and at first thought Tower #1 was falling, since it was damaged first.

Dave had no idea what was happening. He was helping a woman down the stairwell and was on the fifth floor when, with a deafening roar, the building started to collapse around them. As if in an earthquake, the building rocked violently. Suddenly, a wind of hurricane strength knocked Dave to the ground as the compressed air inside the building drove shattered glass, steel and broken wood downward. Up above, he could hear the loud banging as each floor of the one-hundred-ten-story building pancaked down onto the one beneath it. Within seconds, he found himself in what felt like a dark cave. The top of the tower was now the sixth floor, and Dave tried to pull himself free to get there. He could smell the strong odor of jet fuel amid the crackle and urgency of raging flames. Falling debris trapped Dave in what remained of Tower #1 for five hours. Both Towers, for so long an integral part of the New York skyline, lay in ashen piles of twisted metal on the ground.

What Dave could not have known was that within twenty minutes two planes flown by terrorists had purposely crashed into the buildings. What he did know was that he needed to get free to help others, and he was grateful to finally see ropes dangled down from above to pull him up to what little remained of the sixth floor. Stumbling across the scattered debris of the collapsed building in the choking dust he heard small arms fire exploding. Later, he found that it was ammunition stored in the building which was being detonated by the scorching flames. Injured, and temporarily dazed by what had happened, he quickly cleared his mind and thought about Sirius. How would he get to his trapped dog?

Finally back at Tower #2, Dave, covered in ashes, made several desperate attempts to find a way to get to the basement. But firemen and police officers held him back as they tried to secure the area and set up rescue operations. Emotionally distraught, Dave knew further attempts to reach his dog would be futile.

Dave's personal car and police car had both been destroyed in the blast. A familiar policeman arrived and took him to the hospital to be treated for a concussion and leg and back injuries. Dave stayed overnight and was released. For the first time in years he returned home without his dog.

Fall slipped into winter, and even after four months New York workers still faced the grim task of trying to locate victims and to clean up what remained of the two buildings that had fallen into a section now called Ground Zero. Dave monitored the clean up as the long months passed. Finally, a call came to Dave one morning that Sirius's damaged kennel had been found.

With a heavy heart, Dave jumped in his car and raced to Ground Zero to be there for the recovery. The kennel had been found near Dave's locker, and a navy blue uniform shirt Dave had hung on the nearby hook that day was found gently covering the kennel of the deceased dog. When Sirius was brought out, an American flag was

*"I'll come back for you."*

Courtesy of MaryAnn Barbuto

placed over the dead dog to honor the loss of the canine officer for his country. Covered in the flag's brilliant white stars and striking red stripes, the dog was slowly carried from the spot where he died.

During the recovery Sirius received full police honors. The constant drone and grind of the loud machines working in the rubble were silenced. All the Ground Zero workers lined up and saluted, and a heart-broken Dave carried his flag-draped faithful companion from the debris to a waiting police truck. The searchers determined that Sirius had been killed instantly when Tower #2 collapsed.

Dave remembered the promise he had made to the dog that fateful day.

"He waited, and I came back," said Dave in sad reflection.

He knew in his heart that the dog would have waited an eternity for him to return.

At last, Sirius was coming home.

As the city of New York still mourned the tragic loss of life at the World Trade Center, a special memorial service took place three months after Sirius was found. It was held at Liberty Park in Jersey City, New Jersey. The park sat directly across from the World Trade Center site on the Hudson River. Against the now-altered Manhattan skyline, more than two-hundred people and one-hundred K-9 units from across the country gathered in a final tribute to honor K-9 Sirius, Badge #17, of the Port Authority Police Department . . . the gentle dog Dave had called "a big mush." Several of the attending dogs wore badges covered by a black ribbon, matching those worn by their handlers who all grieved for the beloved canine.

The mournful playing of bagpipes echoed through the warming morning air that sunny day, and a twenty-one-gun salute cracked loudly in memory of the friend of the World Trade Center employees. A gentle reading of a poem written by a school teacher from Illinois spoke of the dog's spirit and devotion.

# Sirius

Dazzling sparkle in the distance
Brightest star on earth
Closest to our heart.

You came and shared your light for such a little while

Brought such brightness, gave such joy ...
Now you shine above and watch from distant skies
As the guardian you were, as the guardian you are still.

Companion, guide, protector, friend
Partner and pal on constant alert.
Courageous and cautious,
Patient and obedient,
Strong in spirit, gentle in design,
Quick to defend, eager to follow,
Disciplined for action, poised for careful command.

Sirius ...

Brilliance in the night,
Star of the first magnitude,
Hero of the same
Nine light years away,
Held here in our hearts for eternity.

Sirius ...

friend and faithful partner

Treasured, trusted, and loved,

ALWAYS loved....

Run free across the Rainbow Bridge and in green pastures;
You have done your job well, friend,

Run free, Sirius; run free!

Susan D. Gordon

The excited barking of the gathered police dogs accented the reading as if to concur with its lasting sentiment and soft comforting words.

Sirius's body had been cremated, and a lone pall bearer carried his ashes in a beautiful oaken urn to present to Dave along with the American flag that had covered the dog.

A fifth grade class from J.B. Nelson Elementary School in Batavia, Illinois, had collected money to provide a memorial flag box to hold the cherished flag.

At the conclusion of the ceremony, FBI Special Agent Gerry Fornino, who had been in charge of searching for evidence and personal belongings in the debris, presented Sirius's silver water bowl, which had been pulled from Dave's smashed car. Dave tearfully accepted it. The bowl had been inscribed with Sirius's name, shield number and the words:

*The ashes of Sirius are solemnly presented.*

Courtesy of Debbie Stonebraker

*"I gave my life so that you may save others."*

***Dave Lim accepts Sirius's water bowl, now engraved,***
***which was found in his crushed car.***

Courtesy of MaryAnn Barbuto

Sirius was the only police dog to die on September 11th and was the only dog to die in service during the Port Authority's eighty-year history. Throughout all his years of service, his intelligence and bomb detection ability prevented any suspicious vehicle from entering the area and endangering the World Trade Center employees. It is his lasting contribution. He was the bright shining star that perished with 2,948 people at the World Trade Center that tragic day, each of whom was the love of someone's life. He joined thirty-seven Port Authority police officers whose lives were tragically sacrificed in the disaster. The Port Authority lost three percent of its total force that day. No other police department in the nation's history lost so many officers in one single incident.

After his death, many people wanted to write about Sirius, so Dave was continually asked for pictures of the dog. He realized he had few pictures of them together. After one such request, he decided to offer the picture that had been sent from the White House. As he took it from its frame, he noticed for the first time the writing on the back indicating when the picture had been taken. It read, "White House Photography Office, September 11, 2000," exactly one year to the day before the dog lost his life.

The constellation of Canis Major contains a dwarf star which is a companion in the heavens to Sirius. It is a dim twin star called "the pup" which orbits Sirius every fifty years. Legend holds that the two canines love to play in the heavens and are faithful and loyal friends. And so upon the earth, similarly, such a young pup found its way to Dave to fill the large void. A dog breeder in California donated a young black Labrador retriever named Sprig to shine in Sirius's shadow. Dave accepted the dog gratefully and although he knew that no dog could ever fully replace Sirius, he realized Sprig was a breath of spring after a long winter of pain and horrific memories and a new beginning after the loss of a valued friend.

A portrait of four-year-old Sirius hangs in the New York/New Jersey Port Authority Police Department K-9 Unit as a reminder to all of the eternal and undying love of a dog.

***Captured on canvas for eternity***

Courtesy of Debbie Stonebraker – Stonebraker Art - protected by registered U.S. copyright to Debra S. Stonebraker

With a bond to Officer Dave Lim that can never be broken, K-9 Sirius embodied the faith and trust of all police canines, knowing full well that Dave would come back to get him. And true to the master's word, that is exactly what Dave did.

# K-9 Alley
## "Pride of the Pentagon"

In 1998, an energetic black Labrador retriever joined Heather Roche in Annapolis, Maryland, and was immediately tagged by a search teammate as a "wonder pup." Heather trained search and rescue (SAR) dogs and had several living with her. She named the puppy Alley. The young dog delighted in finding anything Heather dropped, and if that "something" rolled under furniture, Alley

***Destined to search***

determinedly worked her paws beneath the furniture until she could reach it.

If she could not, she stared intensely until Heather retrieved it for her. She was a dog who would not give up.

The little dog continually observed the other dogs' training. Although they were trained to find live persons, they also carried the chilling name, "cadaver dogs." Dogs such as Heather's serve a very special purpose to police departments and rescue groups who are called upon to locate deceased lost loved ones for the saddened families who seek them.

The dogs are trained to locate and follow the scent of human decomposition. What the dogs search for is a "source." That can be anything from tissue, bone, muscle, ligament or organs. Each dog's sensitive nose can detect the scent of decomposition that rises from the soil by using the same principle a dog uses to know where he

***Heather and Alley***
Courtesy of Lisa Kakavas – Mason-Dixon Rescue Dogs

*Highly-trained to assist drowning victim's families*

*Searching for an underwater source*

last buried his bone. They are equally skilled at picking up a scent in water when searching for drowning victims.

By filtering out other odors that interest most dogs, they concentrate on the skin cells that the human body sheds by the thousands. Each cell is covered with bacteria that eats and digests the cell, and the by-product of the process is a gas that the dog can smell whether the cells fall to the ground or are blown on the wind. The cells are so miniscule they can fall between tight crevices, penetrate porous materials or eventually resurface on top of water after they have been deposited and sunk farther down. From each source DNA can be extracted and compared with the DNA of the deceased's living relatives for identification purposes.

Nose to the ground, such dogs can detect clues that will often help solve a mystery or a murder even long after the fact. When the dog catches the scent of death, it will go into a "passive down" indication in which the dog lies down quietly so as not to destroy or damage any crime scene evidence.

Not all dogs have such ability. Through the use of repetitive exercises, the dogs imprint odors of human remains. Some trainers use a manufactured chemical that can replicate some of the odors cadaver dogs must recognize. Heather's dogs learned to "alert" to dirt around graves, to blood and to human bones.

From her earliest days, Alley showed keen interest in such work. She watched her housemates learn the highly-developed techniques. Alley showed an innate driven instinct to search, and soon she began her own training. By just four months old, Alley was showing she could do both live and cadaver searches with not so much as a prompt from Heather. The behavior was unheard of at such a young age.

But when Alley was six months old, she started to limp on her front leg. Veterinary exams showed that she had a condition called FCP, common among Labrador retrievers. A small portion of a joint surface in her elbow broke causing pain and arthritis. This was

*Post-surgery pup*

devastating news for such a promising dog. Another dog handler suggested gently to Heather that Alley be put down. But wishing to preserve the happy little dog's life, Heather scheduled surgery, and the piece of bone was removed. Alley's days as a career cadaver dog were over. Heather would make her a pet.

But Alley would have none of it. From a distance, she continued to watch Heather train the other dogs.

*Searching in the woods gave Alley great joy.*

*Alley in the typical passive down stance.*

Despite her pain, if she sensed a "source" was outside, she could not rest until she was also allowed to find it. Heather tried to distract her with treats, but nothing worked. When Heather took her outside on a lead for bathroom breaks, Alley picked up a scent in the woods and broke her lead to get to it. Heather dragged her away, but Alley broke loose and escaped time and again bounding into the woods.

Once there, she returned to her passive down stance, surrounding the target odor source with her chest and front legs.

But because of her self-initiated search activities, Alley's limp soon returned.

One day a box Heather had ordered arrived. It contained a variety of bones that medical teaching facilities use, which work equally well to train cadaver dogs. Alley limped to the porch and went into her down position near the box. Seeing the dog's passion and drive, Heather knew she would have to let Alley work.

Just two months post-surgery, Alley was enrolled in training classes and performed so well that experts there believed she was a much more experienced dog.

Being able to search kept Alley continually happy. But as the years passed, the work took its toll on her fragile legs. Still plagued by constant joint pain, she maintained her good nature. But romping with other dogs in a muddy creek bed one day caused a more serious knee injury that required more extensive surgery.

*Alley surrounded by her creek buddies, Cassy and Red*

*Post-surgery again, Alley is comforted by her favorite "egg" toy.*

Picking her up after the surgery, Heather loaded the dog in the truck and stopped by a friend's who also trained cadaver dogs. Alley was still mildly sedated from the anesthesia, and Heather knew she could not go far, so she let her out of the truck without her lead.

Alley stumbled in a circle like a drunk and wobbled down the sidewalk. She staggered into a neighbor's yard to the bushes and went into a passive down. Curious, Heather followed her. She had discovered a source the other trainer had planted for her own dog to find. Each time Heather returned Alley to the truck the dog staggered to the bush again. Still totally doped, shaved, swollen and tender, just hours after knee surgery, the smell of decomposition still drove her, and she had to find the source. Without her handler's command, Alley once again initiated her own searches.

"She did not have one good leg to stand on, but she just didn't realize it," said Heather.

Alley's enthusiasm to work masked her pain.

In September, 2001, hundreds of miles south of Ground Zero in New York, a new challenge beyond anything anyone could have ever imagined awaited the team. Alley was called to a place that would test her fortitude and that of all those who worked with her. The Federal Bureau of Investigation sent a letter stating that the Washington D.C. Police Department K-9 unit wanted Alley to join them to search at the Pentagon in Arlington, Virginia. Thirty-two dog teams of "live find" and "cadaver dogs" were called there just five days after a plane flown by terrorist hijackers crashed into the Pentagon killing one-hundred-twenty-five people there and sixty-four more on the plane. Thankfully, Heather's father who worked at the Pentagon had not been among them. "Operation Noble Eagle" was the joint-agency massive recovery effort. Alley and Heather would be an important part of it.

On their first day, September 16th, Heather and Alley arrived at the crime scene very early in the morning. A fenced area surrounded piles of debris moved there from the impact site. The fenced area of the disaster would be home to hundreds of dedicated men and women for many weeks as they participated in the resolute effort to respectfully locate the remains of the victims. A gaping hole in the Pentagon confronted the teams upon arrival. Visible within it were desks, computers and chairs, all appearing to be thrown by an angry hand. The stain of black burn marks spread from the center like an ink blot to beyond two or three times the width of the hole. Within the vast hole, Kleenex, curtain rods, chair arms, glass, metal and cloth could be seen. Twisted metal from an airliner sat juxtaposed grotesquely among the mix of everyday office items.

Everything looked so different from what Heather knew. She had specialized in cadaver training for years, and she had worked small burning plane crashes, but she had never seen anything on this scale. The devastation was so great that it was hard for any human to comprehend it. But Alley could not know what had caused such a scene. She was not caught up in the heart-rending emotion of it all. She knew she was there to follow her nose and search, and that is what she did. The magnitude of the scent of death was overwhelming even for dogs that were used to it. The overpowering smell of jet fuel saturated everything. The dogs caught the scent from every angle on every breeze as they searched through the rubble to find the remains of the people who died there.

The agile teams worked out of the North Parking area where numerous piles of debris had been deposited. Teams that came a long distance slept in tents on cots there. A Salvation Army food wagon, decontamination tent and supply tent sat nearby for all workers. Heather and Alley lived close enough that they could return home after each shift. A tent city called "Camp Unity" was set up to provide for every possible need of the workers and dogs. American companies such as restaurants and businesses provided their products free. Shoes, coffee, hardware, socks, phone service and pet supplies were all supplied by those who wanted to contribute to the search effort.

An orderly plan was in place. First, dogs able to find living people were sent into the area of the crash where they searched for several days. When it was determined there were no more survivors, those dogs were put in their cages, and the cadaver dogs searched the debris piles for evidence and remains.

The level of activity was intense. Constant motion and deafening noise from the lumbering machinery had to be contended with. Dump trucks and Bobcats darted in and out of the area and had to be avoided. There were hazards at every turn. Alley's collar was removed so it would not snag on anything that could cause her injury.

The job was made even more difficult since Heather had to wear a full protective suit, rubber boots, gloves, goggles, helmet and a filter respirator to protect her from the toxins there. Alley wore no protective boots. Had she worn them, she would have been unable to feel hot or sharp objects. Unencumbered by boots, she was able to use her paws for traction on slippery and unstable surfaces. She waded into the greyish-rust debris in places six-to-twelve-inches deep. Pulverized concrete, twisted metal, mangled office furniture, luggage contents, plane fragments and classified material were all co-mingled and buried in the dust. So much was not recognizable.

With measured steps, Alley placed each foot carefully, adjusting each paw if it struck a harmful object until she regained solid footing. Alley was a dog who normally ranged fast and far, so Heather expected to work her on lead, but that was not the case. Alley dragged her to the first pile on the first day and did not let up. She worked with such natural ability that Heather unclipped her lead and let the dog search by her own careful method the rest of their days there.

At the first pile, Alley moved to the edge and began a slow methodical search that Heather could never have trained her to do. Only inches away from the grind and whine of heavy machinery, and ignoring the powerful odor of jet fuel and burned objects, the dog swung her nose slowly over the debris between her paws as she moved forward down a narrow row. At the end of the row, she turned to repeat the search down the next pass. At the end of each pile, she did a perimeter search checking the larger debris that had been moved to the sides. Even when other dogs had searched the piles, and the piles had been raked and sorted thoroughly by several agencies, Alley returned to find extremely small sources that could make a difference to the anguished families waiting for the smallest find for DNA identification.

With each new find, mortuary crews were summoned to respectfully handle the remains. The mortuary staff was at first skeptical of what the dogs could find, but they immediately saw how successful the highly-trained and tenacious animals were, and soon the crews were reading the dogs' signs and acting upon them even before the handlers got a chance to transmit word of each find. Often, if the mortuary workers were not sure about a find, they brought it to a dog for confirmation. Initially, they held it out in front of the dog,

***Debris pile at the Federal Emergency Management Agency
(FEMA) training facility in Maryland. Previous intense
training at the facility enabled Alley to become familiar with
difficult search areas such as the Pentagon piles of debris.***

Courtesy of Lisa Kakavas - Mason-Dixon Rescue Dogs

but the handlers taught them to place it in the pile and let the dog
search their own way for an accurate identification.

The teams searched four-to-five rotations per shift, usually
searching four-to-six piles per rotation. After each rotation, before
they could leave the pile area, they had to go through "decon" where
both dogs and handlers were decontaminated to remove any toxins
that were dangerous to them. Workers in the decontamination tent
dipped scrub brushes into a strong mixture and held the brushes with
bristles pointed upward. Heather picked up each of Alley's legs one
at a time and rubbed them and her paws across the brush to remove
the pungent jet fuel. Then Alley was washed from head to toe. A
second worker sprayed off the mixture with a hose. By scrubbing
the dogs several times a shift and decontaminating their handlers,
most of the harmful toxins were left in the main "hot zone" and not
carried into the sleeping, resting or food areas.

Once Alley was bathed, Heather was decontaminated. Some dogs were afraid of their handlers since they had never seen them wearing a filter respirator before, but not Alley. She took it in her stride. And while other dogs found the decontamination baths distasteful, Alley loved them---until they washed her face. But the water cooled her down after working where torrid temperatures rose from black asphalt like a blast furnace. Alley learned that when she was done with her bath, she could run to greet other workers as she waited for Heather. Workers from a multitude of agencies looked forward to petting the dogs and playing with them, and the hard-working dogs found that the workers would share meals with them. It was a mutually satisfying arrangement that relieved stress for both dogs and workers.

Chaplains were on site, assigned to offer religious counsel to those who worked there. More than once workers, overwhelmed by the incredibly heart-breaking task, stopped to bury crying eyes into the soft warm fur of an available dog who willingly gave comfort. Then both worker and dog would strike out again with renewed purpose and dedication to help their fellow Americans.

Handlers watched for signs of stress in the dogs as well. With most dogs, the stress of such an immense job did not show up until the third or fourth day when their nasal passages became irritated from the exposure to strong irritants such as dust and petroleum products. Many dogs had sore paws and extreme fatigue. Some newly-trained dogs shut down after a few hours working, completely overwhelmed by the circumstances there.

Initially, authorities ordered that the dogs were not to be rewarded as they normally would be when they made a successful find. Possible contamination could make the dogs sick they feared. But without rewards, the dogs soon shut down, and a compromise was reached with the coordinating agencies that allowed the dogs rewards. All the dogs perked up and were enthusiastic to work gain.

When Alley performed well, she was rewarded with pieces of dog biscuits and a soft squeaky red ball, which had to be decontaminated each day so she could take it home.

The rigorous work went on twenty-four-hours a day, seven-days a week, stopping only once for a tornado. On another day a threat to workers kept armed military helicopters flying above the scene for the workers' protection, but the unfaltering teams continued to work through extreme heat and sometimes heavy rain. After long

*A simple red squeaky ball was Alley's reward.*

tedious days, more dogs were brought in, and some stayed in the finest hotels with their handlers.

On one of the last days, two Red Cross workers found the K-9 camp and approached Heather. They were flight attendants and friends of the crew that had perished. The two women collected hair samples from their friends' families. Most families brought in DNA samples from their missing person by bringing in the loved one's toothbrush or hair brush for comparison, in the hopes the dogs would find a DNA match. Their hopes rested with the dogs for the help they desperately needed. The DNA was eventually matched for not only the lost flight attendants, but for everyone killed that day with the exception of the hijackers.

"Operation Noble Eagle" concluded September 27th, 2001. The city of Washington D.C. and the surrounding area was a "no fly zone," and the skies had been eerily quiet for sometime. After the search concluded, the silence was broken by the steady hum of helicopter after helicopter shuttling from the Pentagon to Dover Air Force Base in nearby Delaware, where the precious remains were taken for further identification. Seeing the result of the search at the site, government officials became convinced that the dogs were, and would continue to be, an essential part of any future recovery effort. The dogs had given all they had to give both mentally and physically.

And it was the "happy-to-search" black Labrador retriever who forgot she had four bad legs that helped bring so many who died at the Pentagon home. Anyone watching her flawless work had no idea of her pain. With a high pain tolerance, Alley was so fast and worked so hard, she didn't feel the pain that would have disabled a less-dedicated dog.

Two months after the Pentagon search, Alley tore the other ACL (anterior cruciate ligament) in her knee. Once more she would undergo surgery.

Because of the terror and destruction of September 11th, 2001, the world was, by necessity, suddenly familiar with the words "cadaver dog." Up until that time, the phrase was seldom used even within police departments. The comfort the dogs provided to the families of the victims of September 11th brought with it an acceptance of a term that once connoted a sense of the macabre. After September 11th, the phrase reflected unity and hope for all the families who grieved. The unwavering dedication of so many exquisitely-trained dogs gave gentle closure for anguished families as the dogs brought them the recovery of their loved ones.

The United States Police Canine Association awarded the 9/11 canines that responded to the Pentagon with commemorative medals. The ceremony was jointly held with the Washington D.C. Metropolitan Police Department who operated the Pentagon recovery K-9 cadaver operation and also awarded medals to the dog teams that day.

The following year, Alley and Heather were back at work searching homes and businesses following Maryland's most devastating tornado. Completely focused, Alley trotted along with her head held high until she reached the odor of burnt fuel and gas in the debris. She saw the same grey and rust colors in the debris from the fire that she had seen at the Pentagon. It was all coming back to her. She immediately slowed down to the familiar and intense methodical step-by-step search she had performed at the Pentagon.

"No matter how hard I tried to get her to move on, she wouldn't search normally. She searched like she did at those Pentagon piles until we finally got out of that area. I would have never expected that."

When the Space Shuttle, exploded in February, 2003, Heather was called to east Texas with Alley, spending long days in swampy, wooded terrain. Enduring constant drenching rain the pair helped search for the shuttle crew's remains. Only a few canines in the country were hand-picked for such a sensitive and sorrowful

***Proud to display her medal, Alley symbolizes the remembrance of those who sacrificed all as a grieving country mourned their loss.***

assignment, and Alley was one of them. As the country mourned the horrific loss, the Maryland dog, still in pain herself, once more assisted the grieving families.

In the years that followed, despite several more knee surgeries and balancing on painful legs, Alley's successes continued. So good was her reputation that she was called to a prehistoric Indian village in Mississippi to search the burial mounds and test the ability of cadaver dogs to locate both known and unknown remains there. Excavations in the 1960s had revealed the presence of ancient coffin nails indicating the possibility of burials there. The archeologists had used ground penetrating radar and magnetometers to determine what lay beneath the grassy mounds, and the resulting images led them to believe burials had, indeed, taken place there. When the dogs were brought in for confirmation, they indicated on the very places the instruments detected ancient burials.

At one mound, it was known and confirmed that an historical burial existed there based on coffin nails found in the earlier archeological dig. But, consistently, Alley was drawn to the mound next to it where no previous dig had taken place. The area was so overgrown with vines that Alley could only just begin to penetrate it, but she definitely indicated on the adjacent mound.

It took two years before archeologists secured funding to clear the mound. When they cleared away the tangled vines, the weather turned uncooperative and prevented them from proceeding further. For two weeks afterward, heavy rains penetrated the ground. The ground saturation soon exposed the remains of an ancient Indian child. Only Alley had known the child was there. The cool shading vines had held the scent in the sunshine the day she searched and helped vent it for the dogs to catch. It had taken the heavy rains two-years later to prove her correct. Alley's success at the mounds reinforced the belief that the dogs could positively locate even pre-historic remains.

*At the Indian Mounds, Alley stretches upward to catch the scent she is after, which was held in the bark of the tree.*

In January, 2005, a Medivac helicopter pilot crashed in the Potomac River. Investigative agencies and recovery divers worked in vain for several days but could not locate the pilot. The agencies chose not to use cadaver dogs. They did not believe in the dogs, and they did not want one there. Finally, pressure from the media and outsiders convinced them to allow Alley to search. She made the find in minutes just outside the main search area bringing relief to the pilot's waiting family.

With Alley's immediate success there, those who were skeptical changed their opinions about cadaver dogs and saw the value of using them in future missions. They invited Alley and Heather to attend the later press conference, but with characteristic modesty Heather decided not to attend. She needed no public recognition, but the investigators made sure they mentioned Alley at the press conference giving her full credit for her work to aid the deceased pilot's family.

Four months later, Heather and Alley were called to Bridgewater, Virginia, where they were invited to conduct a presentation on using dogs at historical and pre-historical sites. The archeologists knew that a slave grave had been unearthed when the new road was put in there. They knew the grave had been near the first telephone pole near the field. Curious to learn if more remains were also in the field, they relied on Alley to tell them. When Alley and another dog indicated on a spot near the known location, the archeologist examined the rocks there.

They determined that the rocks and dirt plowed up where the dogs had indicated were not native but brought in and consistent

***In search of a former slave's grave***

Courtesy of Jeff Good, Massanutten Chapter of
the Archeological Society of Virginia

with how slaves would have marked a grave, and that was the proof they needed to confirm their suspicions.

A year later, much to the relief of a grieving family, Alley found the remains of a young murdered girl who had been buried six-feet under the earth under bags of lime. No other dogs could find the child. The parents' pain had lasted for days until the accomplished dog was brought into the case.

August, 2005, Hurricane Katrina, the strongest hurricane ever recorded, smashed into the City of New Orleans and left massive devastation throughout the Gulf Coast States. Alley donned her purple and white vest which identified her as a search dog, and she and Heather left for Louisiana to provide assistance.

The purple SAR K-9 vest, striking against Alley's rich black fur and purple collar, was normally worn for public relations events or when she flew. Heather strapped the vest on Alley on occasion to search along roads or around homes where she might otherwise be mistaken for a trespassing dog, and the reflective tape on the vest

***Readily identifiable as a SAR dog***
Courtesy of Jen Bidner

**Hurricane Katrina**

***Totally exhausted and cover with muck and mud***
Courtesy of Lisa Kakavas – Mason –Dixon Rescue Dogs

allowed her to search safely at night. But this time Alley would wear her vest to travel and join so many other search and rescue teams to jointly work to find an untold number of victims.

Highly-publicized tragedies such as Katrina, the Space Shuttle explosion and the horror of 9/11 often bring the SAR dogs' reputations to the forefront, but on a daily basis their work on less well-known cases performed quietly behind the scenes endears them to their own communities where their only reward is praise for a job well done.

As long as her legs will hold her, Heather is convinced that Alley will continue to search. In the hearts of so many she has helped, canine Alley, of Annapolis, Maryland, and one of the true heroines of the Pentagon search, will always come to mind when someone smiles with affection and says "good dog."

***Good dog. In her senior years but still working, frosted
Alley takes a well-deserved and playful winter rest.***

# K-9 Perry
## "Taking a Bite out of Crime"

"Look what you've done!" exclaimed Deputy Dennis Scheiding of the Preble County, Ohio, Sheriff's Office, when he entered his home after leaving K-9 Perry alone there.

"Shame on you! You know better."

Perry, foaming at the mouth, stood in the bathroom gazing at his handler. It was not the first time Perry had gotten into trouble at home.

Left alone and missing Dennis, the German shepherd, prone to separation anxiety, had wandered about finally making his way to the bathroom. Once there, the lonely dog pushed the door shut behind him. Perry surveyed all he saw there. Up he stretched to the bathroom sink balancing on his back legs. Minutes later, he turned on the water. With a big splash, he pushed a make-up bag that belonged to Gloria, Dennis's wife and a police dispatcher, into the sink filled with water. Next, he found a can of shaving cream and punctured a hole in it with his strong teeth. Immediately, the foamy cream burst from the can and sprayed all over the bathroom, covering walls, floor, towels and tub. In every way he knew, the dog demonstrated his feelings about being separated from Dennis.

There had been many similar incidents with Perry, from destroying numerous pieces of furniture, chewing two plastic dog kennels,

***Dennis and Perry***

dragging a washing machine and later a table he had momentarily been secured to, eating Christmas trees—his reputation at home, and later at work, was taking on epic proportions.

But, Perry was a highly-intelligent dog. He had mastered strict disciplined training in Germany and bore the numbered tattoo just inside his ear that marked him as a well-trained imported dog. He had diligently learned all the required police commands. And he knew he was only to obey them when ordered by Dennis. When Dennis's six-year-old son, Daniel, once argued with a little friend in the backyard, he turned to Perry and screamed, "Stellen!" ordering the dog to chase his friend. Perry looked at him quizzically, turned and walked away. Daniel was marched into the house to be punished, thus ending his brief interlude with German and police K-9 work.

A command of "Fuse" meant Perry must heel, and "Sitz" meant he should sit. "Platz" put him into a down position, and "Blieb" guaranteed he would stay there. Perry responded to "Passauf" when he was required to watch a suspect and "Such" when he had to search. "Nein" meant no, and "Gutbrav," (pronounced gute brauf) meaning "good boy," was the term he sought to hear the most. He was the perfect police dog. He just did not like to be left behind without Dennis.

*Perry trains with a K-9 officer in the purple padded "Barney suit."*

***Being a "gutbrav"***

As highly-trained as he was, it was becoming obvious that Perry could not be left alone to wander the house. His off-duty mischief had to be dealt with. Dennis knew what he was capable of and knew he could no longer give him such liberties in the house by himself.

Sometime later when Dennis and Gloria needed to make a quick shopping visit to the mall, Dennis was determined Perry would not cause more damage.

"I won't be gone long," he told Perry, patting him reassuringly as he put him in his indoor kennel.

Just to make sure escape-artist Perry would stay put, Dennis fastened his hand cuffs to the lead of the dog to anchor him to the cage. Perry seemed content to stay there and wait. Confident the dog could not get into mischief, Dennis and Gloria left for the mall.

When the couple returned, they could not open their front door. Dennis repeatedly pushed his full weight against it. He peeked through the crack to see his brand new couch blocking the door. Beyond it, sat the brand new overstuffed chair. Both pieces, which had just been delivered the day before, were hardly recognizable. The chair could no longer be called "overstuffed."

The stark bare wooden frames of both pieces were all that was left. The stuffing was scattered like cotton all over the room. In his kennel, Perry was lying peacefully on one of the couch cushions he had pulled inside. He had caused massive destruction, but he was content afterward to rest comfortably on the only cushion he decided not to destroy. Ironically, he was still cuffed to the cage.

When Dennis released him, he ran past an overturned lamp and hid sheepishly behind Gloria. But despite his officer's annoyance with him, he was still glad to be back in Dennis's company.

Perry was as professional on the job as he was mischievous off duty. Trained in patrol tactics and lost person and article searches, he was a tremendous asset to the department. His skill at narcotics detection was invaluable. He could easily sniff out marijuana, hashish oil, cocaine, black tar heroin, crack cocaine and methamphetamine, and over the course of his service, he located over two-thousand pounds of marijuana alone. He was a member of the Dogs Against Drugs/Dogs Against Crime Association and was a contributing member of law enforcement dedicated to truly take a bite out of crime.

But sometimes that crime was found in the most unlikely of places.

During a routine traffic stop, Dennis and Perry were dispatched to search a small passenger van. Upon arrival, he spoke with the officer that had made the traffic stop. Inside sat the driver, a prim sixty-two-year-old grandmother and her twenty-year-old granddaughter. The older woman had been acting suspiciously and seemed very nervous after being stopped. The women were both removed from the van, and Perry was called from the patrol car to make a search for narcotics.

Perry slowly walked around the van and stopped when he detected a familiar odor. With much confidence, he sat down at the rear door of the van in a passive alert and waited patiently for his reward, which was a tennis ball. Upon searching the inside of the van, the police officers found two suitcases containing sixty pounds of marijuana inside the rear cargo area.

The drugs were being taken to Columbus, Ohio.

"If you would have gotten me last week," the grandmother yelled proudly as she was taken away, "I had a-hundred pounds!"

The drugs were confiscated, Perry got to play with his tennis ball, and Grandma was taken to jail.

Perry was an excellent dog with children and friendly with students when Dennis searched high school lockers.

***Drugs confiscated after being located in the grandmother's van.***

*Dennis and Perry conduct a locker drug search at the local high school.*

He was an invaluable tool to the school district facilitating identification and treatment for students who had gotten involved in drugs. Perry provided the early intervention required to save the students a lifetime of misery.

After years of training and latching onto the bite sleeve in practice sessions, four of Perry's teeth were replaced with steel ones, at $1200 a tooth, making him ferocious looking to felons and making it even more imperative that he not be left home alone with new furniture.

Once when the Sheriff's Department got an urgent call, dispatcher, Gloria, took it. A violent man violating a restraining order was trying to break into his ex-wife's home with an ax and had threatened to kill her. Gloria dispatched the deputies, including her husband, Dennis, and K-9 Perry. Over the phone she could hear them enter the home. She could hear Perry's intimidating bark in the background as the men pinned the suspect to the ground, and in her mind she could visualize the flash of Perry's sharp, snapping, steel teeth that encouraged the man to comply.

When he worked, Perry was a happy and obedient dog and good company and protection for Dennis. Often his quick and obedient action saved lives.

One warm June night as the pair worked the midnight shift, Dennis was approached by a motorist and advised that there was a man out on the busy highway walking eastbound in the westbound lane at 1:00 a.m. Leaving Perry in the car, Dennis approached the young man and asked him for identification.

"God said I don't have to talk to you," said the man. God says I must go now."

With that, the man darted away, running eastbound again towards two semi-trucks in the middle lane.

"Stop!" Dennis called to the fleeing man.

Both trucks screeched to a stop, averting a collision, and the man jumped onto the side of one of them. The angry driver banged on the door and yelled for him to get off.

With Dennis in quick pursuit, the man leapt over to the eastbound lane and started running westbound against oncoming traffic. Dennis jumped in his car and moved it to the eastbound lane and stopped traffic. Then he and Perry got out. The situation had become desperate as the man remained determine to run about the freeway endangering himself and all the drivers.

Dennis and Perry stood by the car and watched for a moment to see which way the man was headed.

"Preble County Sheriff K-9! Stop! …or I'll send my dog!" yelled Dennis.

"God told me I must go home now," said the man defiantly in reply.

Dennis again ordered the man to stop.

"But God told me to come home now," insisted the man again as he ran.

"Stellen!" commanded Dennis in German, and the dog knew the command well.

With that, Perry sprung forward at lightning speed to apprehend the man. With full force, he leapt upward toward the back of the man's shoulder as he had been taught and spun him around to drag him down. Dog and man rolled over and over into a ditch.

Dennis quickly followed and heard the man's plea.

"God told me I could stop fighting the dog now," he yelled, "GET THE DOG OFF!"

In the glare of flashing police lights, the man was removed from the highway and taken into custody where he could no longer harm himself or others. Not one driver on the roadway had been injured.

Not long afterward, Dennis and Perry were called to a local grocery store where the owner had arrived and had been greeted by the blare of the burglar alarm.

"This is the Preble County Sheriff's Office! Come out now, or I'll send in the dog," called Dennis.

Silence.

At those familiar words he knew so well, Perry was eager to work and started to bark excitedly. Anyone hiding inside was well aware of his presence.

As Dennis and the owner waited outside, Perry was sent in. Dennis followed closely behind working with the dog as they searched up and down the aisles. In the quiet of the store, Dennis could hear Perry's heavy breathing and sniffing as he conducted his thorough search. When he felt confident that the store was secure, Dennis examined the area again looking for anything out of place. Perry was nowhere to be seen.

Just then, Dennis heard a strange crackle coming from one of the aisles. He swung around quickly in anticipation, expecting to see a burglar leap from his hiding place. Suddenly, just ahead, he saw the burglar. It had four legs. Trotting along happily, Perry emerged from the aisle with a big bag of pork skins in his mouth. It was the way he chose to reward himself for a job well done. The grocery owner agreed he had earned them and let him take them home.

Not all calls were false alarms, and not all calls ended so well. On a light rainy evening, the Preble County deputies were called to a heated domestic argument. With Dennis and Deputy Dave Hatfield in the front seat, Perry braced for the emergency speeds he knew would come when the officers turned on the sirens and lights. Traveling at seventy-miles per hour, the men encountered a small car traveling towards them in the opposite lane. Dennis sensed the car was going to make a turn in front of him into a parking lot as it misjudged the distance and speed of the patrol car. Seconds later, it turned. Dennis jammed his foot on the brakes on the rain-slicked road, but he could not stop in time and struck the vehicle hard. Its three passengers were thrown out, scattered about the road like rag dolls. All but the driver sustained serious injuries.

In the police car, air bags deployed with a snap filling the car's interior with smoke. Glass shattered and the sound of metal scraping metal gave evidence to the nightmare that was enfolding. The careening car spun wildly out of control several times and finally came to an abrupt stop. Still inside were the two injured officers covered in shards of glass and stunned Perry who received a bloody nose from the sudden impact. The metal screen had afforded him some protection. Dennis strained to look back through it to check the dog.

"Everything will be alright," Dennis said to the confused dog, trying to calm him down.

Sirens from emergency vehicles screamed toward the crash site, and an Air Care helicopter's whirring blades cut through the night in a low, rhythmic hum. After the passengers of the smashed

*The damaged police car*

car were airlifted to the nearest hospital, the officers' injuries were addressed.

As Dennis continued to hear Perry barking loudly at the arrival of emergency vehicles, he knew his dog was not seriously hurt, and he contemplated his own condition. Emergency squad workers removed the officers from the crushed patrol car.

Separated from Dennis, the barking dog paced and watched nervously as his officer was taken away. Those who arrived afterward were hesitant to remove Perry from the car, because they did not know him and feared how he might react to them in such unusual circumstances. Finally, the dog was removed from the car by an Ohio State Patrol K-9 officer and turned over to local Dog Warden, Tim Vernon, whom Perry knew very well.

At the hospital, Dennis was treated for an injured arm and leg and breathing problems, but he was released the next day. Deputy Hatfield had broken his hand.

Perry was x-rayed and checked at a veterinarian's office, and other than his nosebleed, he was fine and was taken home to Gloria.

The dog leapt and pranced the next day when Dennis arrived home. For four days the two of them rested before returning to the streets of Preble County.

The plea for police help that fateful night was called in by an anonymous person and proved to be a hoax. The deputies had been called out for no reason.

In the years that followed, Perry was called out many more times, and his skillful work brought many successful arrests by the Sheriff's Office.

Perry was retired from the department when he was ten-years-old, after seven years of extraordinary service. He had been deployed four-hundred-ninety-five times and upon his retirement was recognized for his accomplishments.

*Perry of Preble County*

Although many accolades were given to him that day, the best reward that gave the most satisfaction was just being at Dennis's side. He was a dog as hard on crime as he was on couches, and an accomplished dog to be feared by any drug dealer passing through Preble County.

Perry retired to Dennis's home where he had four more peaceful years with Dennis and Gloria. At age eleven, when medical infirmities took their toll, the Preble County dog passed away.

Formally known by his German name, Perry vom Karlmitblick, he worked for the love of his officer, the constant satisfaction of Dennis's company, and upon at least one occasion, a bag of specially-selected pork skins.

*Memories of Perry -- a K-9 to never be forgotten.*

# K-9 Rex
# "MWD"

Military Working Dog. It is a simple military designation given to the four-footed soldiers assigned to military dog handlers. Rex, Latin for king, was treated like royalty by his handler Sgt. Jamie Dana, but MWD Rex was more commonly and lovingly called "Knucklehead" by her.

Jamie joined the United States Air Force and waited four long years to get him, as the Air Force policy required that those interested in K-9 training complete their first enlistment before being considered.

When Jamie was finally selected for the program, she transferred to Lackland Air Force Base in Texas and trained with school dogs that were kept there. Later, after Jamie's departure, Rex would be trained at the same base. In November, Jamie returned to Peterson Air Force Base in Colorado and waited for a dog to be assigned to her. Rex arrived in January, and the match was made.

Military working dogs are trained for assignments wherever they are needed, and like the handlers that accompany them, they are routinely exposed to less than adequate living conditions and very often to extreme danger. After Rex and Jamie became partners, they would test their skills together far from the United States and would come to know that danger.

Rex was placed in his kennel one day in the cool mountainous climate of Colorado and taken aboard a military transport plane with Jamie. Deployed to Pakistan, the two partners sweltered in tents, and the dog handlers had nothing more than primitive outhouses to use. For safety reasons, the handlers were never allowed off base, and no one was allowed on base. The tour of duty in such inhospitable surroundings ended, and after an eight-month respite back in the United States, they were next deployed to the unpredictable and even more dangerous battleground of Iraq.

It took the team a week to arrive in the sun-scorched desert country. Upon arrival there, they adjusted to the forbidding climate and living conditions as best they could and settled in to serve their country.

Jamie and Rex lived in a CHU, a "containerized housing unit," similar to a semi-trailer. In the blistering heat of day, the CHU was

***Jamie and Rex***

***Far from the mountains of Colorado Springs, Jamie
and Rex swelter in a tent in Pakistan.***

their refuge, and the air-conditioning there provided some relief. In the morning or evening when it wasn't quite as hot, they and the three other dog teams assigned there, sat outside the CHU alternating the dogs they brought out for short periods of time. Other than occasional visits to the gym tent or taking meals in the mess hall, the handlers tried to stay inside to keep cool on the oppressive days they were not assigned missions. They found that in Iraq there was not very much to do.

On the hottest days when the temperature could sizzle up to one-hundred-twenty degrees, Rex wore an ice-packed "cool vest" fitted around his chest to lower his body temperature, and he eagerly lapped bowls of cold refreshing water. Luckily for Rex, Jamie's air-conditioned quarters had an extra bed, so he stretched out on it each night, content to sleep at Jamie's side.

Rex was an expert bomb-sniffing dog. He patrolled the dry dusty streets, nose to the ground, carefully sniffing buildings, cars and open areas. He was called upon as needed to support the troops fighting there, protecting them from danger and death. The need was great, and the pair had just completed their tenth mission when they were called to join yet another convoy.

By necessity, they rode in the safety of convoys, each soldier alert to the possibility of attack. The convoy drove cautiously past the worn, sun-drenched shacks where many poor Iraqis lived. The scenery was a far cry from the mountainous landscape and bluish foothills of Colorado. Dingy sheep, thin cows and underfed stray dogs, ready to fight over any edible scrap found, ambled along the roadside in the heat of the day. Shabbily-dressed adults with barefoot children wandered about the outskirts of Kirkuk and stopped to stare at the convoys. The intense and unrelenting sun shone down upon old broken-down vehicles that littered the roadways.

In an often hostile environment, Jamie and Rex searched the typically-humble villages for explosive-manufacturing materials.

Frequently, Rex found containers that had previously held explosive materials. It was hard to say who had used the containers and for what purpose. The mere presence of such containers did not bode well for U.S. troops. But the armed convoys continued. Nothing was ever routine on a convoy in Iraq, and each journey out was increasingly fraught with danger.

On June 25, 2005, Jamie called Rex into a Humvee and convoyed with Army soldiers from the 116th HHC Idaho National Guard near the city of Kirkuk. Jamie sat behind the driver, and as Rex sat at her side watching intently from behind the passenger's seat, he barked sharply as he viewed each new passing sight.

Traveling into the unknown, danger could be sudden and unexpected.

But some dangers were harder to detect than others.

Just after one o'clock in the afternoon, an improvised explosive device (IED) buried in the roadway detonated with explosive fury when Jamie's Humvee rolled over it. The damaged vehicle flipped twice and then rolled over three more times.

Instantaneously, the roof gunner was ejected and landed on the roadway in serious condition. One of the soldiers in the front seat sustained a broken wrist and the other soldier, broken ribs. Rex was blown out of the Humvee onto the debris-covered roadway. Jamie was by far the most critically injured. The vehicle had quickly become an unrecognizable burning mound of twisted metal.

Jamie lay in the intense heat on the dirt road lapsing in and out of consciousness.

Rex was nowhere to be seen.

They had been in Iraq just three weeks.

Forty-five minutes elapsed before help arrived.

Barely alive, Jamie was taken to the field hospital tent at Kirkuk where she arrived less than an hour after the blast. After an evaluation there, the medical staff determined her injuries to be massive and her

*All that remained of the Humvee's back section where Rex and Jamie sat. It had flipped twice and rolled over three more times.*

Courtesy of Major (Dr.) Paul Morton

***Point of impact***

Courtesy of Major (Dr.) Paul Morton

condition grave. Her doctors thought for sure she would die. Jamie arrived with internal bleeding that eventually required nineteen blood transfusions. She sustained a fractured spine, and her pulse stopped twice. In addition, her internal organs were pushed up into her lungs. Critical and alone, in a country far from home, the young woman fought for her life.

Jamie's lung tissue was severely injured, so much so, that the tissue responsible for blood-oxygen exchange was destroyed. It was a race against time as Jamie's lungs quickly filled up with fluid from the injury. She required a more powerful ventilator than the ones at Kirkuk in order to keep her lungs open, and decisions had to be made quickly.

*Anesthesiologist, Dr. Scott Janus watches as Dr. Craig Pack administers oxygen to Jamie, and Dr. Paul Morton, to his right, closely assesses her situation.*

Courtesy of Major (Dr.) Paul Morton

Initially Jamie could speak but not for long

"Is my dog dead?" she weakly asked.

She continued asking about Rex, and Major (Dr.) Paul Morton, with the 10th Medical Group, who cared for her, repeatedly told her he had heard the dog was fine. But no one knew for sure. Due to anterograde amnesia, common after such trauma and head injuries such as hers, Jamie didn't remember anything and continued to ask about Rex until she could ask no more.

Suddenly, Jamie's oxygen levels dropped so low that Dr. Morton had to anesthetize her to allow the ventilator to breath for her. He administered IV fluids and transfusions since her blood pressure was very low due to severe internal bleeding. With great concern, the doctors debated performing surgery at Kirkuk but decided to

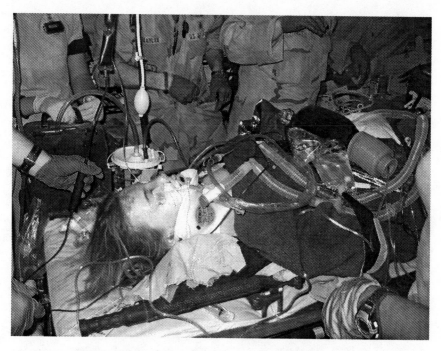

*After working heroically to save Jamie, the trauma team at Kirkuk prepared her to be airlifted out.*

Courtesy of Major (Dr.) Paul Morton

***Medical personnel carry critically-injured Jamie to a
waiting Black Hawk helicopter for evacuation.***

Courtesy of Major (Dr.) Paul Morton

airlift her down to Balad where they had better ventilators and more
surgeons.

Seldom did the team at Kirkuk send their own doctors with
patients on the evacuation helicopters, but Dr. Morton was so
concerned with Jamie's blood pressure and oxygen levels that he flew
along with her. As her condition deteriorated during the flight, he sat
poised to administer CPR. Dr. Morton reverted to unconventional
methods just to maintain her oxygen levels at minimum required
levels. Against the loud whir of the helicopter blades and huddled
over a young woman whose condition had become increasingly
grave, Dr. Morton fought to save her. With an insufficient ventilator,
he hand-squeezed oxygen to her severely-damaged lung tissue
through the bag valve mask device she wore. By all rights, he knew
she should have died during the flight, but he continued to work, as

she continued to fight, and when the chopper at last touched down in Balad, she was still alive.

Still burdened by the possible loss of her dog, Jamie was next flown from Balad, to Landstuhl, Germany, for additional surgery.

Throughout her ordeal, she never stopped asking for Rex, refusing to believe he was dead. They had arrived in Iraq together, and she envisioned them leaving Iraq together. The loss of Jamie's constant companion made her injuries all the more painful to bear.

Jamie remained hospitalized in Germany for a week, and on July 3rd, she was transferred to Walter Reed Army Medical Center in Washington, D.C.

Day after day, Jamie struggled to regain her health and some normality in her life. Each day she endured pain, but she had a strong will to live, and it was that will that had brought her a long way. Her world was one of I.V.s, medications, physical therapy and constant pain. Some days she was clear thinking, and other days she was not. And through the prolonged recovery and the long bedridden hours her thoughts in her lucid moments returned to the dog she had once loved and had left behind in the precarious war zone of Iraq. Rest and therapy would make her well, but nothing would fill the void she felt without her beautiful knucklehead, Rex.

Visitors came and went, including singer, Travis Tritt, and Secretary of Defense Donald Rumsfeld. Jamie was awarded a Purple Heart in a ceremony in her hospital room, and she was promoted to Technical Sergeant in a pinning ceremony there.

She was grateful for the attention and the outpouring of love for her, but she still mourned for her lost dog.

In small increments of success, Jamie got through the therapies that would teach her to walk again and to eventually take care of herself. It was a hard-fought daily battle.

One day as Jamie stared at the same four confining walls of her room wondering what her future would hold, her parents and eight-year-old brother, Brody, each of whom had kept a constant vigil at her bedside, returned for their visit. They told Jamie she should expect a visitor.

After greeting her family and wondering what they meant, Jamie heard a familiar sound. A dog panted in the hallway and toenails clicked noisily out in the hospital corridor. The sound stopped just outside her door. The eyes that had been dulled by sadness and pain brightened in recognition. Jamie's countenance evolved into a giant grin as a furry head poked through the doorway.

With all the strength she could muster, Jamie took a big breath and whistled.

At the familiar tone, a large German shepherd responded and raced into the room.

"Rex!"

Rex jumped up on her bed, and in his excitement to be petted got tangled in her IV line, but nobody really cared.

The dog Jamie had loved and missed surrounded her.

Still somewhat dazed from medications, Jamie hugged and kissed her beloved Rex, and he nestled into her familiar but now frail arms, his soft fur warm and welcome against her skin.

Amid tears, hugs and licks, Jamie cradled the big dog, and it slowly sank in that he was truly back. Iraq had not taken him from her.

The medical staff knew that he was not only her partner but an essential key to her recovery, and they were grateful to have him there.

Over and over, Jamie's family had told her Rex had been found and was alive, but through the fog of severe injury and the dark days isolated in intensive care, heavily sedated, she could not comprehend what they were telling her.

Now, it was all too good to be true.

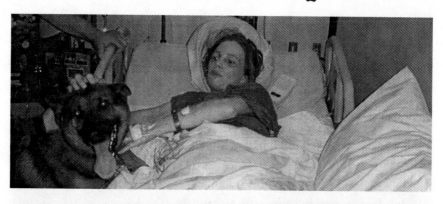

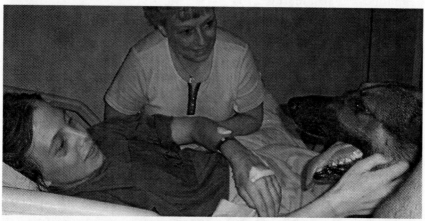

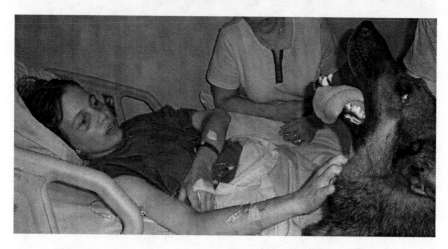

*Flown in from Iraq, Rex is reunited with Jamie at Walter Reed Hospital as Jamie's mother, Karen, looks on.*

Courtesy of Lee Chambers, AFSPA

Rex had been flown from Iraq to Andrews Air Force Base where he stayed at the kennel there. Official policy dictated that he was required to return to the United States after his recovery. Once he was well, he was not put back into service in Iraq. Other handlers kept him busy with training, but with his own handler gone, he was no longer of use in Iraq.

It was eventually decided that the best job he could perform was to comfort Jamie and remain at her side through her ordeal.

Jamie was just learning his story.

At the time of the explosion Rex was thrown free of the Humvee, ran from the vehicle and continued running down the road. In pain

***Left behind in Iraq, Rex no longer had a handler to work***

and confusion, Rex ran amongst the stray dogs and native people who had seldom seen a dog like him.

When word got back of the explosion, a convoy was alerted to look for him. Not long after the explosion, another convoy that was coming back to help Jamie's convoy found him wandering the roadway and picked him up. Besides bumps and bruises, he had a minor burn on his nose and cut on his foot. The frightened dog had been shaken up badly as he ran from the explosion. But Jamie had been evacuated with such speed, that there was no time to tell her he had been found. Given her critical condition, she would not have processed the news had she heard it.

As she recovered, Jamie made a formal request to the Air Force to retire her dog and grant her the right to adopt him. She argued that they were inseparable, and he was vital to her recovery.

But the Air Force was technically prevented from honoring Jamie's request by Title 10 US Code 2583, a law that permitted Military Working Dogs to be released only after they were no longer useful to the Department of Defense. Since it took an Act of Congress for a military working dog to retire early, Congress needed to act quickly, or Rex would be taken away from Jamie and brought to the military dog training facility at Peterson Air Force Base back in Colorado Springs. Rex's case was presented to several lawmakers who lobbied on Jamie's behalf to change the law, and the urgency of the issue was stressed.

In the meantime, Jamie was released from Walter Reed Hospital at the end of September. During her time there, Rex was a frequent visitor as he was brought from Andrews Air Force Base by a friend. His visits were the most healing therapy Jamie could receive.

While everyone anxiously waited for Congress to act, Air Force officials agreed to an unprecedented request to permit Jamie to take her assigned military working dog home with her as she recovered.

*Sweet quite moments shared at home*

"She and Rex went through that together," said Air Force Brig. Gen. Robert Holmes, "and I think our leadership feels that they need to heal together."

Jamie's family drove her back to Pennsylvania where she and Rex spent a month.

In the quiet of her parent's home and the familiarity of her old room, Rex jumped into bed with Jamie staking out his permanent sleeping place. There they would heal emotionally and physically and await the crucial decision.

While there, Jamie contemplated her future.

She knew her military days were over as her injuries would force her to retire from military service. After her recovery, she dreamed of becoming a veterinarian. It was still unsure what her future held, but as her health improved, she began to make her plans.

"I pray every day," she said, "that Rex will be a part of them."

Although Rex retained his loving personality, he hated to have people look at him through a window or peek at him through a door.

He became sensitive to anything that moved outside the vehicle he rode in, and when he saw anything move, he started barking ferociously. He had his own adjustments to make.

Weeks went by, and still no official word had come from Washington. After a month, and still walking with a cane, it was time to return to Peterson Air Force Base. Before she left Pennsylvania, Jamie's town of Hazel Hurst gave her a spirited parade. She and her family and Rex piled onto her father's hay wagon and rode through the streets to the cheers of her community. Then she boarded a commercial flight back to Colorado after Thanksgiving with Rex traveling by her side in the passenger compartment.

A Congressional vote was scheduled for December 12th before Congress left for the holidays. Both Houses of Congress approved legislation that made it possible for Jamie to adopt Rex. The Department of Defense Appropriations, H.R. 2863, Conference Committee Report, lines 7 through 12, was amended to include language that empowered the Secretary of the Air Force to make Rex available for adoption by his handler, TSgt. Jamie Dana. President Bush signed it into law on December 28, 2005. The law was the best Christmas gift Jamie could have received.

Due to the nature of their incident, the Congressional Defense Committees changed the law in 2006 defense legislation to allow military working dogs to be adopted by their handlers following a traumatic event.

The Air Force officially retired Rex at Peterson Air Force Base in January, 2006. Jamie was a proud participant in his retirement ceremony. After recognition of his distinguished service, she received a certificate of adoption and a certificate of retirement for Rex which were both signed by the Secretary of the Air Force, The Honorable Michael Wynne and the Air Force Chief of Staff, General T. Michael Moseley. Rex was officially hers.

***Rex is officially retired.***

Courtesy of G. Dennis Plummer, U.S.A.F. Photo

***At long last Jamie receives Rex's retirement
certificate from Major Paul Cairney.***

Courtesy of G. Dennis Plummer, U.S.A.F. Photo

While still in Colorado, Jamie and Rex welcomed a special visitor. Dr. Paul Morton had returned from Iraq and paid a visit to his former patient.

***Jamie and Rex await the arrival of Major (Dr.) Paul Morton.***
Courtesy of TSgt. Matthew Gilwreath, U.S.A.F. Photo

***Major (Dr.) Paul Morton meets Rex for the first time***
***when he visits with his miracle patient, Jamie.***
Courtesy of TSgt. Matthew Gilwreath

In early February, 2006, a dog was one of First Lady Laura Bush's special guests during the President's State of the Union address. TSgt. Jamie Dana accompanied that special dog. Nicely brushed and groomed for the occasion, Rex sat beside Jamie once again, this time in a shiny government vehicle. They met Mrs. Bush at the White House and rode with her to the Capitol to hear the President's speech from the First Lady's box. After the President's State of the Union address, he and his wife posed for a formal picture with Jamie and Rex.

**President and Mrs. George Bush pose with Jamie and Rex.**
Courtesy of the White House Press Office

*Jamie presents a picture of herself and Rex to Pennsylvania's Representative, John E. Peterson, to show her appreciation for his leading efforts to propose legislation.*

Courtesy of MSgt. Jim Varhegyi, U.S.A.F. Photo

*Jamie and Rex with Representative John Murtha of Pennsylvania, Chairman of the House Appropriations Defense Subcommittee, who was instrumental in getting the appropriate legislation passed.*

Courtesy of Msgt. Jim Varhegyi, U.S.A.F. Photo

***Senator John Warner of Virginia, former Chairman, and
later the second-ranking Republican of the Senate Armed
Services Committee, greets Rex and Jamie at the Capitol.***

Courtesy of Msgt. Jim Varhegyi, U.S.A.F. Photo

TSgt. Dana was the first military working dog handler to be allowed to adopt her dog from active duty. It was the United States Congress that, with much compassion, recognized the urgency of her request and in a magnanimous, non-partisan political gesture proved they understood the true love of a dog.

Far from the excitement and honors of the nation's capital, Jamie quietly completed her military service and retired. She and Rex returned to the serenity and rolling hills of Pennsylvania for good where Jamie bought a small farm.

Whether a veteran, future veterinarian or farmer, Jamie's future remains bright along side her once lost and ever-faithful friend, a canine knucklehead that changed the laws of a country and brought a frightened young woman with enormous fighting spirit through her darkest hours.

# Tailpiece

## THE CREATION OF MAN'S BEST FRIEND

*God summoned the beast from the field, and he said, "Behold man is created in my image. Therefore adore him. You shall protect him in the wilderness, shepherd his flocks, watch over his children, and accompany him wherever he may go - even into civilization. You shall be his companion, his ally, and his slave.*

*To do these things, I endow you with instincts uncommon to the other beasts; Faithfulness, Devotion, and Understanding surpassing those of many himself. Lest it impair your courage, you shall never foresee your death. Lest it impair your loyalty, you shall be blind to the faults of man. Lest it impair your understanding, you are denied the power of words. Speak to your master only with your mind and through your honest eyes.*

*Walk by his side; sleep in his doorway, ward off his enemies, carry his burden, share his affections, love and comfort him. And, in return for this, man will fulfill your needs and wants which shall be only food, water, and affection.*

*So be silent and be a friend of man. Guide him through the perils along the way to the land I have promised him. This shall be your destiny and your immortality."*

*The dog heard and was content.*

Author Unknown

203

# About the Author

Marilyn Jeffers Walton is a graduate of The Ohio State University. She has written six books for children, including the successful Celebration Series for Raintree-Steck-Vaughn. Her book, *Chameleons' Rainbow*, won a Children's Choice award in 1986. She is the author of *Rhapsody in Junk—A Daughter's Return to Germany to Finish Her Father's Story*. She and her husband, a retired Miami University professor, raised three sons in Oxford, Ohio, where they currently reside.

She has always loved dogs including her own canines, Willie, Smokey and a German shepherd mix and K-9 wannabe, Sandy.